Steelhead

To the four special ladies in my life:

To my wife, Frances A. Thornton, who, for thirty-five years, has been a loving, patient, and understanding fishing widow.

To my mother, Constance I. Thornton, who promoted the world of fish and the memories in the written word.

To my daughter, Catherine F. Thornton, who shared many special outdoor trips.

To my granddaughter, Linda P. Thornton, who already has salmonid fever.

Steelhead

Barry M. Thornton

hancock

house

ISBN 0-88839-370-9

Cataloging in Publication Data
Thornton, Barry M.
    Steelhead
    ISBN 0-88839-370-9

    1. Steelhead fishing. 2. Steelhead fishing—British Colum-
bia—Vancouver Island. I. Title
SH687.7.t56 1995 799.1'755 C95-910742-8

Cover Design: Myron Shutty
Editor: Karen Kloeble
Production: Myron Shutty, Sandi Miller, and Nancy Kerr
Cover photo: Barry Thornton

Published simultaneously in Canada and the United States by

HANCOCK HOUSE PUBLISHERS LTD.
19313 Zero Avenue, Surrey, B.C. V4P 1M7
(604) 538-1114   Fax (604) 538-2262

HANCOCK HOUSE PUBLISHERS
1431 Harrison Avenue, Blaine, WA 98230-5005
(604) 538-1114   Fax (604) 538-2262

Contents

One

The Steelhead Trout
Oncorhynchus mykiss

The Supreme Sports Fish

Steelhead, the "Prince" of Salmonids, is the trophy trout which river anglers in the Pacific Northwest acknowledge from experience is the greatest freshwater game fish in North America. My first experience with the awesome power of this trophy was typical to that of every angler who first hooks a steelhead. My drifting float, holding fresh roe just above the bottom of the stream, had submerged and instinctively I lifted the rod to set the hook. I can still recall the immediate disappointment when my hook struck solid but nothing happened. I was certain that I had hung up on that inevitable snag which lies in every pool. Impatiently, I began to strip line through my fingers, as one does with fly line, in an attempt to loosen the hook. But, when I had gathered no more than five feet of slack in front of me, the line suddenly streamed through my fingers and a fish of unbelievable power charged to the head of the pool and then turned and raced out the tail end. Having only fly-fished with single action reels during the previous ten years, I had instinctively tried to handle the spinning reel and monofilament line as one does a regular fly line. The result was predictable. I lost the fish and the fifteen-pound-test nylon line shredded my index finger and sliced two great gashes in my hand. Thoroughly stupefied and nursing a hand that hurt like blazes, I resolved then and there to put one of those magnificent fish in my creel!

Success came so quickly to me that first year that I am certain the angler's guardian looked down kindly as I stumbled and splashed, learning the skills of river wading and the infinite variables of river lore.

I was fortunate to have a patient teacher during those early trials. I am reminded of him when I angle in pools we once drift fished together, or stand where rivers once flowed and fish once struck. As he taught me, so have I taught many others since then.

In those early years, the hope of catching the limit was the

8

extrinsic motivation that prompted trips through freezing rain, hail, floods and snowstorms, tens of miles from the nearest telephone.

But, the intrinsic motivation was always there and it soon blossomed; along the angler's trails; through trilliums and dogtoothed violets; with the sights of river otters frolicking in streams, and in the first blush of pink wild currant flowers in the spring! It also led me to see pristine elk trails and centuries old cedars, cougars, mink, martens, and even the rare Vancouver Island wolf.

While these two separate motivations combine in infinite ways to make anglers as individual as the casings on caddis-fly larvae, there is still a common bond which draws all steelheaders together. This bond is the unbelievable power of a trophy trout! It is an awesome power that will whip any fishing rod into a complete bow in a fraction of a second!

The steelhead's incredible size magnifies itself when he leaps, spraying columns of water upward and making waves that rock the very banks of the stream. The minutes, the quarter hours of inevitable dogged fights test angler and tackle to the extreme. Any weakness in tackle or technique results immediately in a lost fish. The steelhead's totally unpredictable power may expend itself in silver flashing leaps through the pool or in a rocket torpedo that jets out of a pool taking a hundred feet of line in one dash. And, even if harnessed, the rippling muscles of that torpedo power spray water, sand, and gravel at the arm-weary and emotionally exhausted angler.

In my earlier search for this river trophy I used a seasonal approach. But, I quickly learned that every month on Vancouver Island is the month to fish steelhead. Boxing Day marks the "traditional" opening day for winter steelhead but this has now changed with many rivers having sizable runs in October and November. Today, heavy November and December rains bring fresh runs into virtually every Island stream.

Vancouver Island anglers are blessed, as many stream choices have summer and winter steelhead. At least a dozen steelhead streams are accessibly located within an hour's drive of any community. Further afield, throughout the Island, there are over 150 major steelhead streams and at least 2,000 creeks, many having individual runs of steelhead. Almost all are accessible by major public or private roads. In total, they provide extrinsic and intrinsic qualities equal to all the desires of every individual steelhead angler.

Early winter steelhead have a special appeal to the ardent steelhead angler, but, be warned of an irresistible affliction. Not only is December the beginning of a new season with all its anticipation of tackle-breaking, water-walking, trophies, but, it is also a time to renew old acquaintances with the river.

Truly, it is the lure of the river more than any other factor that draws the early steelheader to "his" stream and "his" pools. It is the vivacious animated water—the variable flows, volatile and fickle; the multiple signs and multi-faceted delicacy of wildlife; the challenging power of the current and the undulating streambank. This is the appeal of the river! To each angler it's embrace is individual and unique, and it has an eternal hold on the ardent steelheader.

The longing to return to the river grows irresistibly as the angler watches every change and shift in the weather, waiting for that perennial moment when his instinct and passion drive home once again to favorite holts.

When late November and early December bring their gusty southeasters and prolific rain, the enticement is overpowering. Unlike most Islanders, the ardent steelheader starts each morning wistfully checking the northwestern sky and weighing the possibilities of rain. His is not the sane conforming wish for clear skies and sun but, rather, a rain-maker's desire for storms. Perfect weather for the steelheader would see a heavy rain storm on Monday and Tuesday, receding on Wednesday, with a cold snap on Thursday to check the headwater run-off. Friday would remain cold with a light drizzle beginning in the late afternoon and continuing over the lower reaches of the river throughout the weekend. The cold snap on Thursday would put a bite to the river water, further triggering the steelhead's migration instinct. The cloudy, overcast Friday evening would hasten the fish into the river where they would hold in the various pools of which the angler is the master. Cloud and light rain on the weekend would have fresh winter steelhead moving through the river with every tide change. Many of these fish moving through the river would provide fresh action at each pool throughout the weekend.

There is one final attraction for the ardent early winter steel-

10

header and that is the possibility of lunker steelhead. These trophies, which reach beyond the five-kilo mark, have incredible warm water power and are often the first runs to enter the early streams. These fish are often "ripe" when they first enter fresh water, sporting dominant rainbow stripes and pink, but not dark, lateral sides. The rivers are still warm this early in the season and this gives the fish increased potency. This, together with their great size, will leave many anglers standing incredulously on the riverbank, unable for many minutes to repair broken tackle and equipment after one of these trophies has torpedoed out of the pool in the high-fall freshet, wrapping line around stumps, snags, and river bends as it streaks downstream.

To fish for steelhead is one of nature's premier gifts to the angler. Those who have experienced the force of a river current pulsating against leg and thigh while they attempt to beach a water-walking, chrome-bright steelhead, know the thrill, the tension and the indelible memory such an encounter brings. The steelhead, this "Prince" of the salmonids, is a worthy challenger, an adversary that by his very existence ensures that water will always remain fresh and clean and man will protect the watershed headwaters of every stream, the natural environment so vital to the well being of all living things.

Steelhead Trout

The steelhead is an anadromous rainbow trout which, through evolution, has developed a life history dependent upon both salt and fresh water. The eggs hatch in late spring or early summer depending upon the water temperature in their home stream. The fry then spend an average of two to three years in fresh water and then migrate to salt water as a smolt. As young adults, they live in the North Pacific ocean for an additional two, three, or four years before they return to their native river to spawn.

After spawning, the steelhead trout reverses the physiological changes which occur during the spawning period and returns to salt water. After one or two years, they will return to freshwater to spawn a second, and in very rare cases, even a third time.

As a member of the trout and salmon genus, *Oncorhynchus*, the steelhead is an effective predator near the peak of the fresh- and salt-water ecosystem. As a predator, their early life in the stream and their later life in salt water is devoted primarily to the endless search for food. They likely live a solitary life until the spawning urge sends them back to their home river where they may seek the company of other steelhead.

While in the stream as a fry, the steelhead feeds on everything and anything that has movement, from a struggling insect to a bouncing salmon egg. The limited food in the fresh water environment naturally limits the steelhead's growth. As a two- to four-year-old smolt ready for migration, the average length of these juvenile fish is under fifteen centimeters. Once they have reached the sea, however, myriad aquatic life provides an almost limitless supply of food in the form of smaller fish, squid, crustaceans, euphasiids, and others. It is during this salt water period that the tremendous growth of the steelhead occurs.

When the steelhead returns to his natal stream to spawn he will average seven pounds. Should he return to spawn a second time, and approximately 20 percent do, he may have increased his weight from the rich ocean feed. The lunker or heavyweights which weigh twenty-plus pounds are usually steelhead that return for their first spawning after staying at sea for three, four, or even five years.

Upon returning to the stream to spawn, two major physiological changes occur in the steelhead. First, the roe or milt sacs enlarge while the other internal organs, particularly the stomach, shrink to allow room in the body cavity for these growing reproductive organs. Paralleling these physical changes are other chemical and hormonal changes which eventually cause the fish to cease active feeding.

The second physiological change relates to body color and shape. In body shape, the male develops an elongated and pronouncedly hooked lower jaw called the kype. The female, on the other hand, alters her external shape very little during the spawning period.

The body color, more pronounced on the male, will change to a crimson red along the lower sides and belly. It has been suggested that the color change has a two-fold purpose: first, to aid in species and sexual recognition and second, to incite aggression toward other males.

The migration habits of steelhead are a complicated interaction of stream temperature and flow, air pressure, water clarity, cloud cover, and daylight. In my opinion, the combination of daylight, the timing of the run, stream temperature, and flows are the most important factors affecting migration and hence angling success. My experiences have shown that steelhead do not enter a stream if the water flow is too low, possibly for fear of exposing themselves to predators.

As a sea-run fish, steelhead, following that instinctive daylight factor, will arrive at the estuary of their native stream and join the other individual steelhead waiting for either the temperature triggering factor or a relatively safe flow of water. When this occurs, steelhead will begin their upstream migration to the spawning waters, along with the others who have been waiting, starting a "run of steelhead" in the stream. Although steelhead may start the run in association with others as a school, it appears that they migrate as individuals until they reach their spawning area.

While migrating, winter steelhead will occasionally ingest

worms, salmon eggs, nymphs, and other stream biomass material. However, they generally cease feeding when they enter fresh water to spawn. If, on a rare occasion the winter fish actively takes a lure or bait, it may be that the hormonal changes from the developing roe or milt sacs or the warming fresh water have not yet inhibited the feeding urges. This is one basic area where I feel that summer and winter steelhead differ. It has been my experience that summer steelhead will actively feed in the stream while winter steelhead do not.

The summer-run steelhead appears to be a distinct sub race of steelhead. Studies have shown they will not interbreed should they inhabit the same stream. Different from winter steelhead in their spawning migration, they enter their home stream as adults from June through October. The only certain identifying features are: the size of the milt or roe sacs, which are thumb size when they first enters the stream, or the time of the year they are caught, from June through October. Although the summer-run enters the stream earlier than winter fish, they will not spawn until the following winter-spring season, the same period when winter steelhead spawn.

Fluorescent red and orange are acknowledged as the most effective colors to use for catching steelhead. Recalling the crimson sides of a spawning steelhead, it would appear that the red artificial lure may exaggerate the sexual aggressiveness of the fish and cause him to take the lure.

During his upstream journey, self-preservation and the urge to arrive at the spawning grounds pattern his migratory habits. During daylight, with its increased predators and increased exposure, he will seek a resting area in the deeper waters of river pools or white-water slicks with the reassuring current stroking each side of his body equally.

When he has completed spawning, his body chemistry reverts to its former state and, as a kelt, he often becomes a voracious feeder trying to restore sapped body energy to keep his body functions active until he reaches the multitude of feed available in salt water. He is very vulnerable at this time and, having used his reserve body fat while spawning, he is certainly not as desirable as a table fish.

Recently, steelhead lost their unique North American nomenclature (*Salmo gairdneri Richardson*) as a result of a decision by the

American Fisheries Society's Names of Fishes Committee. They concluded that the Asian name *mykiss*, historically applied earlier to the Asian (*Kamchatka*) steelhead race, would now take "nomenclatural priority" and will be the "proper scientific name for this species." Also, this committee concluded that there was "no biological basis" for distinguishing rainbow trout from Pacific salmon at the genetic level, hence, all trout and salmon "of Pacific lineages" are now considered to belong to the single genus, *Oncorhynchus*, originally used only to refer to Pacific salmon. As a result, steelhead now come with the scientific label, *Oncorhynchus mykiss*!

Wildlife Wonders on a Steelhead Stream

As my fly drifted over the shallows of the Upper Island Pool on the Campbell River, I became aware of a seagull behaving in a strange manner on the other side of the river. I reeled in my line and paused in my fishing to watch this seemingly unnatural behavior. First the gull would swim upriver and then, like a Merganser, dive deep. It was obvious that he had found something he wanted, but I was astounded to see him finally lift up the heavy carcass of a large chinook. With unerring skill the bird rafted the carcass downstream, through a fast white-water stretch of water and then, with intrepid skill, pulled the carcass up on a river snag and began to feast. As I began once again to cast to my steelhead run I applauded the skill of my coastal companion.

Winter steelheading provides a wealth of wildlife experiences for those who will pay attention to the signals of nature. In recent years, as I have taken the fly rod more often than the float rod on my river excursions, I have found myself able to take in more detail of my surroundings, not having to concentrate on my drifting float. I have always been amazed at the numbers of wildlife species I have seen along each riverbank. Vancouver Island is in fact a rather barren wildlife area. We have no skunks, no porcupines, no chipmunks, no bobcats, no lynx, no large mammals like the moose or caribou, sheep or goats, no native rabbits, no coyotes, and no grizzly bears. We also have no poisonous snakes and, except for devil's club and the rare mushroom, no serious poisonous plants. A rather barren land you might say. No, to those who would sit on a riverside log and observe we do have many riverside wanderers.

In my river trips, the most common mammal I have seen has been the Columbian blacktail deer. The Vancouver Island herd is estimated at between 200,000 and 400,000 in any given year. Next to the Queen Charlotte Islands, this is the highest density in North

America. We do not have the large mule deer nor do we have the whitetailed deer, although the flashing tail of the blacktail is occasionally mistaken for the whitetail. Deer tracks on river trails and clear sandy beaches add an ingredient, an entity to those special pools where I have fished.

Every river trip draws my attention to these wanderers as I check their tracks on the riverbank trails or on the parchment sandy beaches near steelheading pools. My experiences with the blacktail deer have been highlighted by much contact. Likely, the most dramatic was the time I found myself wading out towards a logjam in the Eve River and dragging a drowning deer to shore. While this was physically exerting, the sight of a cougar chasing a deer along slippery beach gravel on the Gold River and finally stopping when the deer swam downstream and across the river, left me applauding but emotionally drained. A similar situation occurred on the Oyster River when I watched a panic-stricken doe escape a small pack of very dark Vancouver Island wolves by dashing across the river in a section where the wolves floundered. I am certain it was this pack of black, snub-nosed young wolves which gave me a start I will never forget.

I had been concentrating on my float while fishing a particularly productive pool on the Oyster River early one morning in late April. On the far side of the pool was a high, steep, loose humus cutbank. I had rolled a bright fish in the deep water at the far side of the pool and was persistent in my casts to that very specific site. All I can remember is that the pack of wolves, in unison, began sharp, short barks accompanied by threatening growls. Startled, I looked up at the top of the bank and saw these black, large-tailed but snub-nosed teenagers telling me in no certain terms who owned this river. Apprehensive, but not yet frightened, I stepped back up to the beach and stood while they snarled and barked at me. In moments, however, I heard a sharp bark from a larger wolf standing in the shadows of a spruce tree behind them and watched in amazement as the pack, as one, turned and faded into the thick salmonberry thicket. It is a moment of wildlife contact which is firmly etched in my special river contact memories.

How often I recall the frightened blacktail deer doe that raced under my fly line while I was concentrating on the slight nips, which

I was certain was a steelhead, following my fly downstream. The doe had appeared out of nowhere, leaping and slipping in great bounds along the open gravel beach. That something was chasing her was obvious even though I never saw her pursuer. It seemed she was mesmerized in her terror for even when I stepped back from my stance on the riverbank she never flinched. To avoid a sure collision with my low fly rod, I lifted the ten-foot tip high as she passed only feet from where I stood. She leaped into the river as one would visualize a great black lab would do on a mallard retrieve. The water sprayed out in a wide swath, then she was swimming for the far riverbank. When she reached the shallows her terror was still obvious. She made great leaps in the shallows, then was in the woods and disappeared. It all happened in less than a minute but it was a remarkable sight.

One winter friend that I have always paused to enjoy is the water ouzel or "Dipper" as it is more commonly called. This tiny slate gray bird is hilarious with its jerking-bobbing antics as it balances on streamside rocks. I have often watched it dive into the river and like a large bubble of air, pop to the surface upstream from where it first dove in. The prolific caddis fly larvae on coastal streams are the focus of this underwater feeder who actually walks on rocks upstream underwater collecting his food.

Mink are another common animal which I have been fortunate to see many times. I recall one incident when I was sitting on a streamside log when this brown slim, sleek creature suddenly ran across the toe of my wader. I don't know who was more startled, the mink or me, when I instinctively, like being hit on the knee with a doctor's hammer, kicked up my foot throwing the mink in the river. But, the most dramatic scene I witnessed with a mink occurred one morning on the Little Qualicum River. I was fishing that very productive run just above the Trestle Pool late in December. A few fresh steelhead were in the river and I had just beached a bright small buck. Re-tying my terminal tackle, I sat on the riverbank opposite a shale rock wall full of squawking, mewing seagulls. I spotted a sleek mink gliding down one ridge of shale above a young gray-feathered herring gull. In a matter of seconds the mink leaped forward and bit the gull on the back of the head. The gull flopped over head first into the river. With weak flapping wings, it drifted downstream while the mink followed on the rock beach ledge. In moments, the gull had drifted over a small falls, wings no longer moving, and the last I saw, as he disappeared downstream around a bend, was the mink patiently keeping abreast of the gull waiting for it to come up against the beach.

One river trail friend for those steelheaders who will pause on angling trails, is the winter wren. This thumb-sized, sassy ball of feathers is a certain companion wherever you travel. on coastal streams. My fondest memories of these characters include the "chit-chit-chit" cry that follows my river wanderings. I know that whenever I come to shore to walk a trail, rather than wade the river, this noisy friend will be there scolding me for interrupting his far more important activities.

While Vancouver Island does not have the nervous chipmunk, we do have our fair share of red squirrels. Like the winter wren, this bustling forest folk greets the steelheader on river trails throughout coastal forests. I am constantly amazed at the energy these fist-sized mammals exhibit: dancing along logs, rapidly chewing on various evergreen cones and then, after dashing up a tree trunk, standing on a branch and with a raucous chatter, while flipping their tails skyward, they challenge all intruders. The forest would be a lesser place without them.

Last spring, while playing a steelhead on the Little Qualicum, I looked upstream to spot three river otters swimming down to the pool where my steelhead was fighting. I had a light leader and could not force the fish to the beach, but it was not necessary. The three otters, heads up and ears alert, swam down river on the far side of the pool apparently taking no notice of the flashing, struggling steelhead between us. Throughout the years I have had the pleasure of meeting and watching river otters on a number of occasions. One memory that stands out was the time I found a family of five using a snowbank on the Oyster River for a slide. For an hour I watched these sleek and skillful clowns climb the bank, slide down into the water, crash into each other, roll on the snow and carry on as if they did not have a care in the world. It was a memory equal to any steelhead I have ever beached.

In another chapter I speak of the beaver, that very important steelheader's engineer. While I have seldom seen these industrious workers on the stream, the evidence of their work floats down the river every freshet. Their skill, creating wading staffs, is equal to the finest carpenter and their ability to clear streams of heavily branched fallen trees is unsurpassed. I know my steelheading experiences have been enriched by their industry and I thank the River Guardian for giving us such a welcome stream companion.

In this short chapter I have only touched on the many experiences I have shared with wildlife on steelhead streams. Wildlife wonders are there all around us as we search for our Prince of salmon. It seems that each trip I take brings a new experience which compliments my angling pleasures. These have provided me with a richness, an indebtedness that has no price. This is the angling experience that we all, as steelheaders, search for every trip that we take.

Two

Fly-fishing for Steelhead

Fly-fishing for Steelhead

Standing near the beach in knee-high water in my chest waders, false casting, I finally laid my rainbow-pattern fly on the water at the usual forty-five degree angle upstream, mended the line as best I could in the fast current at the head of the stump pool, and then, watched as the line swung in a growing crescent downstream. It stopped! There was no feeling of a traditional strike, that take from a feeding trout, rather, the line simply stopped! After a moment, I was certain I had hooked a snag in the bottom of the river, having felt that same immovable pull many previous times.

Still cautious, however, I stepped back to get a better pull on the line and was just lowering the rod tip to point at the snag when the chrome-bright doe exploded up out of the pool in a series of poetic leaps. This began one of the most memorable fights that remains firmly etched in my memories of the many steelhead I have been fortunate to beach.

On the first leap, the #10 twenty-foot sink-tip fly line streamed through my fingers. The initial shock of the leaping fish had set the hook well in the side of her mouth and the fight was on! I remembered, I don't know how, to bow to her with the rod when she leapt high a second time. I am certain it was from pure reflex, but it was enough to save the eight-pound test leader. When she hit the water after that second towering leap she headed straight upstream, out of the white water at the head of the pool, and up through the shallows, heading for the lone, half-buried cedar stump after which the pool was named. Only a few years previous, the stump had rested at the head of the pool and formed the base for one of the best steelhead slots in the river. Flash floods in recent years had moved gravel downstream around the stump and had shifted the main pool further down.

Fortunately, the stump was at least fifty meters upstream and the doe soon slowed, then halted behind a large white boulder. Here she tested the pull of the hook, moving her head from side to side.

Suddenly, she reversed, and headed straight down through the shallows into the white water at the head of the pool. I reeled frantically as she streamed downstream, watching the odd upstream facing crescent of line while I tried to put her back to the reel. For a long moment the line appeared to go slack, then, I had her to the reel once again!

What followed was the typical dogged, thrashing, rolling, twisting fight of a fresh-run, fly-caught winter steelhead as she tried in vain to rid herself of the hook. Soon, however, I had her over to my side of the river. She struggled even more in a sudden short spurting fight so common to big fish when they are held in a shallow run of water which they dislike. I moved slowly downstream until I was able to hold her in a small backeddy. Here, vanquished at last, she rolled on her side and I eased her up on the rocks at the shore. She measured just short of a meter in length, weighed just over eight kilos and was as silver as any trophy steelhead fresh from the sea.

This special fish came to me the first year I seriously fly-fished for steelhead. Since that memorable day I have followed these trophies in many pools, through many waters and along many river trails. I have been fortunate to beach many fish and each, thankfully, has provided exciting memories.

It is the rare winter steelhead that will actively strike at a fly. Rather, the fly must be presented in such a way that it drifts in the same manner and at the same depth as the resting fish. This is the secret, the truism of winter steelhead fly-fishing! This factor also holds true for summer steelhead, however, these latter fish are prone under certain conditions to actively "take" your fly.

Recognizing this truism, it is obvious that fly-fishing tackle is of utmost importance. A vast array of fly lines are now available, with major companies like Fenwick and Cortland making substantial improvements each year. Fly line purchases should be weighed against the water conditions in which you fish, with the weight of line and rod carefully balanced to the American Fisheries Tackle Manufacturers Association (AFTMA) scale (recently changed to the Sports Fishing Association). A #10 fly line must be used with a #10 fly rod. I have found that even one scale of difference, a #9 with a #10, a #9 with a #8, does affect my casting. But, I have also found that there is considerable difference between companies and that a

#7 rod built by one company will often cast a #8 line while this may not be the case with another company.

Fly lines should be measured for pleasure and efficiency during a full day's casting. Powerful light weight graphite rods are now available and do increase the line weight possible for a day's casting. But, does the pain of the one o'clock to ten o'clock wrist snap and power cast measure up to the pleasure of the day's outing? My personal preference is with a matched #8 outfit for the average-sized Island streams for both summer and winter steelhead. On larger river waters, like the Stamp, Gold and Campbell, I will regularly use a #9 or #10 outfit, switching to the #8 and less challenging water when I tire.

In order to sink my fly to the fish, I have spent many years experimenting with a variety of balanced outfits, from #7 weight to #12 weight, from shooting heads to level lines, from leadcore to heavy-grained lines, and from spit shot to weighted flies. Initially, I was blessed with occasional tantalizing success. Now it is a time of deep pleasure with increasing success punctuating each day's outing.

I have found that short leaders, about thirty centimeters in length, are the best for they let me know and control where the fly is during each deep drift. These short leaders also keep my fly down, enhancing the sink-tip lines that I prefer. I have often wondered why some steelhead fly-fishermen go to great lengths to find the fly line which will take their fly down to the fish only to counter the effect of the line with long leaders which float the fly high above the steelhead. The only exception to the short leader is when I am dry fly-fishing for summer steelhead on clear coastal streams.

In many water situations I will use weight to ensure that the fly is drifting at a level with the fish. In shallow water, about a meter in depth, I will use wet fly hooks to keep the fly down. But, as the water deepens in runs or pools, I will use a weighted fly and/or a small split shot a few centimeters from the fly. I have never yet hooked a fish with a split shot resting against the eye of my hook, although I am certain that anything is possible. When the split shot begins to slide down the leader to the fly I simply untie my fly, slide off this used split shot, retie my fly and add a fresh split shot. I have tried a variety of methods with split shot including the use of a small dropper leader with the split shot attached. However, the best method I have found, which still allows for a natural cast, is the distribution of the split shot over the main leader up to a maximum of three split shot.

The fly reel used by the fly-fishing steelheader must have a number of attributes. This is likely the most important part of your tackle and unlike a simple trout fly reel, which is normally used just to hold your fly line, the steelheading fly reel is used to fight your fish! It must be able to hold about 100 meters of level wind backing which in turn must be secured to your fly line in such a manner that it will run smoothly through the eyes of your fly rod. Most steelhead will eventually take you into this backing! This is a fact for which steelhead fly anglers must be prepared when they hook these trophy trout. The reel must also have a drag-braking system which can take the sudden rush that a steelhead will give. I have had a number of steelhead actually tear out the drag on some reels and now I use only the strongest quality reels I can find.

Over the years I have come to believe that the fly used for winter steelhead is not as important as the fact that the fly must be presented immediately in front of the fish. Winter steelhead rarely feed actively while they are on their upstream spawning migration in the stream. They are accessible to the fly-fisherman only during those times when they rest in the tailout of pools or in favorable runs and slots which provide conditions in which the fish chooses to rest. It is during this time of rest, the momentary pause in the spawning urge, that the fly-fisherman has access to the fish.

Summer steelhead, on the other hand, are very selective about the flies they will take. Select a few of the proven patterns like the Western Bee, the Skunk, the Bomber and the Purple Peril for your kit and carefully observe patterns that other anglers use on each river. It is known that certain patterns work better than others on individual rivers and it is only local knowledge that will ensure you are fishing with an effective pattern.

Unquestionably the angler must have confidence in his fly! He must know that the fish will take it if the presentation is correct and if he is to spend the many hours casting that is required between takes. Truly, winter steelhead fly patterns are as varied as the number of individual steelhead fly-fishermen. All, however, are basic attractor flies using pinks, reds, and orange colors and often tinsel.

During the past few years I have focused on the simple *Thor* pattern. This fly uses a red or orange fluorescent colored body with polar bear hair tail and wings as its primary materials. A simple fly, but recognized throughout the Pacific Northwest as a successful pattern that is a real confidence getter.

Once the angler has determined that he will search for the majestic steelhead with a fly; has purchased balanced fly line and rod; has filled his reel and tied/purchased known successful flies; then the next most important aspect of this tackle is the presentation to the fish!

The steelhead fly-fisherman needs mathematical precision for each stretch of water he fishes. It is crucial to visualize the pool bottom where the fish will lie and create an imaginary grid using underwater white or colored stones and constant slicks and white water breaks as markers. Once the grid is formed a simple but rhythmic system is required to cover the full area. The "3x3 system," one cast up, one cast across and one cast down followed by three short steps downstream, is one such system which soon becomes second nature to the fly-fisherman.

Recognizing how the stream will belly the line and cause the fly to streak downstream until the belly is straightened, the angler needs to make the water work his fly. Without question, the dead-drift action of your fly is the most effective for steelhead. This can be perfected with the line mend following your cast.

To mend your line, immediately after the fly has settled, lift your rod tip up and roll the fly line over on the water upstream. This extra fly line, zigzagged on the river surface, retards the action of the surface water on the line before it is able to apply a constant pressure, hence, creating a belly and racing the drift of the fly. With practice and water-reading lore you are able to determine just how great a mend should be applied after each cast. Eventually this, like the "3x3 system," also becomes second nature to the river fly-fisherman.

This past season I found an ideal steelhead fly run on one river which constantly held fish. It is a wide, shallow area with a few large boulders which created slicks and side channels which in turn resulted in holding runs in the shallows. Many times I worked the area thoroughly with a fly, hooking one, two, and even three steelhead. It was a stretch of water of which poets would write. As the season advanced, my curiosity got the better of me and I wondered if there were still catchable fish in the run. Thereafter, when the fly action stopped, I used my combination outfit and worked the runs thoroughly with a float and egg imitation lure. Invariably, on the first drift through with the Gooey-bob lure I would hook a steelhead. Subsequent drifts would often result in additional hooked fish.

Why didn't they take the fly, particularly as I had systematically cast and dead drifted the fly through the exact same waters? One can but theorize and I feel there are a number of reasons why the fish didn't strike.

Likely the action of the fly when it was drifting with the fly line was not the same natural action of a drifting lure fished with a float. Often I have hooked a fish when I have float fished a fly through waters that I had previously fly-fished unsuccessfully. In this particular run I can recall a number of fish hooked within moments of the fly hitting the water after the cast. I feel that the fly line had not yet been subjected to the pull of the current and the fly was at that time drifting naturally.

I have felt strikes when the line was at its full swing, but rarely do I recall hooking a fish after what I feel was the time when the line was caught by the current. I have tried another technique, with some success, which seems to give me a few feet more of dead drift. With this system, I pull the fly line towards me with a full rod lift and a short mend, after the river has bellied my line. This effectively slows the fly creating a short natural drift partway through my covering of a section of water. Lures like the Gooey-bob do drift along the bottom of the stream, bouncing downstream in a natural way at the same level where the fish lie. The weights on the main line used when float-fishing catch on the bottom gravel and delay or jerk the lure along. This is the action which seems to cause the steelhead to strike, likely because it is similar to the bottom insects and eggs upon which the steelhead ate when a fry in the stream. Will the fly ever be as effective as float-fished tackle? I rather doubt it, simply because the fly cannot reach those deep, secluded resting areas where steelhead tend to hold. But, in shallow waters, I do feel that the fly can be as effective if fished by a determined fly-fishing steelheader.

It has been my experience that most fly hooked steelhead will immediately bolt from their lie and, more often than not, explode into the air in an attempt to shake the hook. This is contrary to the action of most lure-hooked steelhead who tend to sulk at the bottom of the river or make fast rushes in the stream. I feel the difference in behavior is a result of the heavier fly line over which the angler has not yet gained control on the initial strike. The fly line will have bellied by the time the angler registers the strike and this growing downstream crescent of line swings the fish downstream and forces it to leap on its first run. Unquestionably, this is the crucial moment! I have watched many flies snap back at my rod tip, torn loose from the fish's mouth because I failed to bow when he leaped. It is a moment not for the weak of heart, for these are big fish!

Concentrating on one specific run this past winter, I tried a number of new casting ideas which I am certain gained me many a hooked fish. The run always held fish but while each strike was basically different they did fall into four basic forms.

The first was the sudden halt strike! This strike usually occurred when the fly line had been cast upstream and the fly had not yet drifted level with the beach where I was standing. The pattern for this strike was the snagging action on the take, as if the fly had hooked on an underwater obstruction and was hung up on the bottom. Usually, it took a measurable moment, it felt like an eternity, before the fish moved.

The second was the immediate strike! This occurred within seconds of the fly landing in the stream on the cast. In this particular strike, I am certain that the lightly weighted fly and sinktip line sank immediately in front of the fish, who took the fly by instinct.

The third was the full-reach, long-swing strike! This take occurred after the fly line had lost its mend and was just beginning the swing while at full extension.

The fourth was the rare retrieve strike! This particular strike came while I was stripping the line back after its swing through the run. Surprisingly, these were often bright fish who seemed to actually come from another section of the run to take the fly.

One particular large male fish stands out from the many I caught from this run. He was a classic example of the sudden halt strike and deserves further detail.

When I lifted the rod tip following the sudden halt of the fly line swing at the tail of the pool, there was no give. I tested the tip for a moment and then walked upstream in an attempt to dislodge the fly from what I thought was a river bottom snag. When nothing happened, I wrapped the fly line around my right forearm, pointed the rod at the snag and began to walk further upstream. This time I had walked only a few steps when the line began to tug in my hand and I knew it was "fish-on!" In a panic, I quickly unlooped the fly line from my forearm just in time to watch a great buck steelhead leap into the air. He hit the water with a resounding smack and ran out to the middle of the stream. Here, he leapt once again and then began to sulk. I blessed the #12 test leader and felt a wave of relief when I realized how close I had been to losing this trophy.

What began then was a long, slow, tedious struggle which saw the fish repeatedly leap with the bright red Thor fly showing on the side of his mouth. Then, there were those sulking, erratic head shakes, which forced me to palm the single action reel to hold him in the pool.

The run was shallow, ideal for fly-drifting, but it was tricky holding water for a struggling fish. Where I was standing was a smaller backeddy at the edge of an upstream shallow. It was the only deep water with conditions which would hold a tiring fish.

I found it impossible to reel the heavy fish to this area because each time I tried a steady reel it jerked with his struggle and he fought to remain in the main river. So, instead of forcing this, I simply walked upstream with the rod pointed at the fish, sliding him around boulders and steering him to the backeddy. When at last the fish eased into the backeddy, I slowly reeled in the slack line and walked back downstream.

Throughout the walk upstream, the fish continually arced his body against the pull of the line, using the full benefits of the varying currents to add strength to his pull for freedom. But it was to no avail. Once he was in the backeddy, I began a steady pull towards the beach. The buck repeatedly arced his body using a form of centrifugal force to assist his swim out to the main current, but this time he was too tired for any long run.

When I finally had him near the beach, the tip of his tail surfaced and gave away each of his attempts. In a few moments he rolled on his side and I slowly eased him up on the beach. He lay quiet on his side, with the bright red Thor fly hanging from the edge of his mouth almost matching the prominent rainbow streak along his side. He was a very large buck just beginning to darken to his full spawning dress.

He continued to lie quietly while I adjusted my camera and took a few photos. When I reached down and grasped the barbless hook fly it literally dropped out of his mouth. A moment or two more in his struggle and he would have pulled it free. I moved him off the shallow water near the beach and turned him on his belly, watching the gills slowly work the life giving oxygen back into his system. He soon realized that he was free and with a powerful snap of his tail, which sprayed at least a gallon of water all over me, shot out into the main current and disappeared.

My first summer steelhead on a fly came from the Marble River. It was not a big fish but it surfaced and sucked the fly from the surface. In the clear summer waters every action of the fish was visible, from its slow rise out of the bottom of the pool to its nonchalant take of the Western Bee fly. I can still see the open mouth, a white silhouette in the green canyon waters, as the fly disappeared.

That first fish came surprisingly easy. We had driven to the river while on a North Island exploration trip and it was only minutes after we arrived that this fish took. Our day ended with three fish, all chrome-bright with that faint pink rainbow hue so common to summer steelhead.

I count that trip as my first summer steelhead fly-fishing experience. It was quickly followed with July and August fish from the Stamp, the Kokish, the White, the Puntledge and the Gold. When the Campbell River Tsitika runs began in the 1980s, I found myself concentrating on the most productive "fly only" section of the upper river with incredible results. The Tsitika summers were on average large steelhead, many weighing in the high teens. They were explosive fish and tested leaders, lines, and rods to the extreme. I was fortunate to hook many fish and these honed my skills and gave me that vital essence of confidence to pursue these wonders of summer rivers.

I have heard some anglers refer to the Campbell River as a "poor man's Dean," a reference to the wild steelhead caught in that mid-coast river. But, while the Dean may be a famous summer steelhead river, the Campbell is fabled! It is the Campbell, more than any other river in recent years, which has given steelheaders the opportunity to experience quality summer steelhead on the fly.

The management program which has given fly-fishers the opportunity to fly-fish for large summer steelhead is detailed in my story of the Campbell River. For me, the Campbell River offered that special opportunity to experience quality and quantity summer steelhead fly-fishing. I remember one particular day when I was experimenting with a new fly pattern, the Pink Campbell. Pink is a very effective steelhead color which seems to excite even the most reluctant summer fish. On this special day, after fly-fishing the midisland run with no success, I decided to tie on a weighted pink fly combination, tied with a pink polar bear hair tail, a salmon-colored Frostbite body, a hot pink plastic chenille head, all tied with silver thread on a #1 O'Shaughnessy Mustad 34007 silver hook. I moved up to the midportion of the run and, incredibly, a bright summer took on my first cast. It was a powerful fish and took a good half hour to finally beach and release. Excited by this change of fortune, I waded back to the lower reaches of the run, took a few false casts then laid my sink-tip line out over the deep emerald-colored water. The fly could not have drifted more than a few meters when a second bright summer doe hooked herself. This was another powerful fish, but came quickly to my side and allowed an early release. One would have thought one fish was sufficient with a pattern change but that was not the case. While the next three fish required that the fly be in the water on more than a single cast, when the afternoon waned I had hooked and released five good fish and lost two others. Could it be that a fresh run had just entered the pool; could it be that the first fish disturbed the others and placed them in a position which my fly could access, or could it be that the pattern was what the fish wanted? Whatever the reason, I have since made extensive and successful use of that "Pink Campbell" pattern in all Vancouver Island rivers.

March is that special month which epitomizes all that is the essence of the winter steelheader. It is that month when all streams have runs of chrome-bright winter fish; when stream flows are constant and dominated by that magical steelheading olive green color; when the "whump, whump, whump, whump" sound of the drumming "willow" grouse announces the awakening of spring. It is the time when stream waters begin to warm and steelhead become accessible to the winter steelheading fly-fisher.

But, while March is the month of the winter steelheader, October is the month of the summer steelhead fly-fisher! This is the glorious month when all summer steelhead streams have their full complement of summer fish. It is in October that low clear waters hold undulating green-backed, torpedo-shaped trophies in canyon pools and river riffles. It is the month when crisp mornings stimulate the angler to travel, to move from pool to pool experiencing the moods and contours of these special streams. Wildlife is in abundance in this season (blacktail deer on nuptial missions) and falling deciduous leaves blanket the riverbank and swirl in backeddies. It is a month of color so magnetic that no other can compare.

April is the climax of the winter steelhead season. The last major winter runs of these trophy trout move into their natal streams in surprising quantities with almost every tidal change. Some streams are finished by April as far as fresh run fish are concerned, but they are few and are generally the smaller creeks having extremes of summer and winter flows.

It is in April that most steelhead spawn. As a result, there are many dark fish in the streams and many kelts migrating downstream to reach the ocean. Most anglers release dark fish for aesthetic reasons and the kelts out of empathy. Between the number of kelts and fresh fish still entering the river, the angler is provided with supreme sport unequalled in any other month of the year.

During April, many steelhead anglers who have worked the streams all winter with conventional tackle switch to fly-fishing. They have learned the "slots" in various sections of their home rivers and know that in these slots there will be steelhead!

Slots are very specific lies with constant stream flows and shallow depths that regularly hold steelhead. Only a few steelhead runs maintain these ideal conditions but these are usually guaranteed to hold fish late in the season. In the smaller streams, or streams abused by logging or road construction, these slots shift after every major high water. However, a number of these slots remain the same even after years of changes in other sections of the river.

It is on these slots that the fly-fishing steelheader should concentrate. He may work a few of the other runs or pools where he has taken the occasional fish, but he only has moderate faith in the productivity of these areas. However, he does know that they are secondary holding water and that there is a chance that a fresh fish has passed there or better yet, that there may be a "wild" kelt holding on its downstream migration.

For some reason, completely foreign to my experiences, kelts are looked upon by some steelheaders as having very poor sporting qualities. On the contrary, kelts have always provided me with explosive and, in many cases, startling battles!

As a rule, they are voracious feeders on their downstream migration and strike at most flies presented. In many cases they will dart from their lie in some section of the pool, striking the fly with a ferocity that is only equalled by the resulting battle—should the angler's reflexes permit him to hold the fish.

Those annual showers common to April also give two basic advantages to the fly-fishing steelheader. First, the cold winter waters begin to warm, activating the steelhead into striking at the fly. During winter months, flies must be presented directly in front of the fish. Even then, he will generally only mouth the offering. The angler, during the winter, has to be constantly alert to the slightest take on his fly. In the spring months, however, warmer water will cause the fish to move from his lie and actually strike at the fly.

The second advantage to the fly-fisherman comes from the freshets caused by these spring showers. These freshets cloud the stream for short periods, forcing the fish to hold at the tailout of their run. This is usually in very shallow water, difficult for drift fishermen to reach and almost impossible for float fishermen to cover. However, the fly-angler can cover these areas with deadly accuracy!

Hatchery steelhead introduced to many rivers are now providing "bonanza" summer and winter steelhead angling experiences for many steelheaders. These "urban" steelhead have led many anglers to experiment with tackle with the result that there are now a large number of dedicated steelhead fly-fishermen on rivers. These experienced steelheaders know intimately the slots in their home stream. They know how to take advantage of special stream conditions which are the major factors in the steelhead fly-fisher's formula for success!

Fly-fishing Skills

Fly-fishing for steelhead is a constant search for mastery of stream knowledge and river-fishing skills. We are fortunate that coastal streams provide many opportunities for developing successful stream fly-fishing skills because of their maritime climate and the cornucopian quantities of salmon at varying months of the year: Sockeye in July, Pinks in August, Chinooks in September, Coho in October, Chum in November and Steelhead all months of the year.

Fly-fishers new to this coastal fly-fishing wealth must realize that for anadromous salmon, including summer and winter steelhead, they face a completely new set of factors compared to fly-fishing for feeding trout.

The first and the most important difference is the fact that steelhead *do not feed* when they return to the river to spawn! Why then do they strike at a lure? The only acceptable answer appears to be because they are what they are—steelhead. Yes, some summer steelhead will feed; yes, during warm winter rains (April showers) some winter steelhead will ingest worms and insects. But, this is not the feeding we associate with the daily activity of resident river trout. Rather, it is the associated activity of the species! They strike because they are what they are! It is for this reason that rainbow trout, both inland and anadromous, have been transplanted to locations throughout the world. They are the classic sporting trout!

For those who wish to pursue specifics, there are numerous physiological reasons for this nonfeeding behavior on the part of steelhead. The most obvious is that when they return to spawn, their stomach shrinks to provide space in the body cavity for the female and male roe. This alters their body chemistry and inhibits a daily feeding schedule or need. One interesting report I read told of a summer steelhead that was held in a hatchery pen for eleven months without feeding and yet only lost a few ounces in weight. A sure sign of the adaptability of this species.

Once the fly-fisher new to coastal streams has accepted this quantum difference between anadromous trout, those fish that journey to the sea and return only to spawn, and resident trout, those that remain in their home river throughout their life, then that fly-fisher is ready for consistent success with these trophy fish.

One of the first skills the coastal stream angler learns is the difference between pool types and their resulting holding water for resting steelhead.

From my travels and fishing experiences I would classify stream pools into three main types: "dogleg," "crescent" and "run." The dogleg pool is a sharp right or left angled pool, with a decided ninety degree angle turn. The crescent pool is one with a slow gentle curve, usually with a steep bank on one side. The run pool is one having a deep depression in the middle, but with the river neither turning right or left. Within each of these pools, regardless of type, there are three main holding areas for salmon and steelhead: the white water head which holds about 10 percent of the fish, the main pool which holds about 40 percent of the fish and the tailout which holds 50 percent or more of the fish.

But, there are additional subtle areas which should be evident when a pool is being analyzed. One is the inner slack area caused by a deep depression immediately following the pool head and slanting towards one side. Usually this is an obvious area because of the finer stream bottom material of silt and sand. Another common area is the big rock slick, an area resulting from one or more large boulders in the pool. Another is a bank root or log edge, which results from streamside undermining. A further area is a "V" midstream slot caused by sloping instream gravel beds. One final area is a pocket pool caused by boulders wearing on sandstone stream bottoms.

The fly-fisher, upon reaching a pool, needs to plot a specific plan for fishing that pool. When I first reach a pool that is unfamiliar to me, I take time to consider a number of factors, usually in the following order:

1. Where is the best location for a holding fish? Where are the secondary areas?

2. Which is the best side from which to cast my fly?

3. When I have hooked a fish where will I beach it?

4. What obstacles does this pool contain, obvious and hidden?

5. What happens to my backcast; do I need to throw a roll cast; will my fly tick beach rocks and break the point?

Once I have answers to these questions, I will, if necessary, wade across the stream to be on the best casting side. Then, I will start my fly-fishing at the head of the pool.

Steelhead are resting fish when they have returned to their home river to spawn. I know that I must present my fly immediately in front of a fish if he is to strike. If the fly drifts too high, or too low, or, if the fly travels/swings too fast, there will be no strike. My presentation must be perfect for these are very selective fish and, even then, I know that the odds are that the fish will not strike. But, I also know there are a few "catchable fish" in every pool!

Catchable steelhead are a phenomenon likely unique to this one sporting salmon species.

I can remember fly-fishing a pool on the lower Big Qualicum River a few years ago beside and opposite a number of other fly-fishers. In the clear water we could see about forty bright, fresh-run winter steelhead pooled but not taking any flies. However, there was this one identifiable fish, with a large open wound, which was hooked on four separate occasions in one short hour while not another fish struck at the smorgasbord of flies presented to that visible school. This one particular steelhead, dubbed "Ol' Seal Bait," by the first angler that released it, had a chunk of flesh taken from it's back, likely as the result of a bite from a harbour seal which are very common at the estuary of that river. There were at least eight anglers at all times fly-casting in that bridge pool, using every technique possible; from dry flies to skaters, shallow sink wet flies and heavily weighted sink flies. Every twenty minutes or so one angler would shout, "Fish on!" and the rest of us would reel in our lines while the lucky angler reeled in the identical steelhead that had been beached before. It was uncanny how that one fish repeatedly took a fly while the others simply swam with closed mouths. Why just this one fish? I am certain this was the catchable steelhead, that one in 5-to-15 percent of steelhead in each river which will strike at flies and lures.

To get to these few catchables that are the bread and butter fish of the steelheader, I have found it necessary, particularly for winter steelhead, to use a fast sinking, sink-tip line preferably of twenty-foot length. I do carry five-foot, ten-foot and thirty-foot sink-tip lines which I will use on occasion, either on smaller or larger streams, but I would recommend the twenty-foot as the most effective fly line. I have found that the twenty-foot sink-tip fished with short two-to-three-foot leaders gives the best presentation for my flies.

When you are dry fly-fishing it is easy to watch your fly, to see how it performs as it drifts, skates, or swings across the pool. This fly movement is just as important for the wet fly-fisherman and must be visualized and understood to develop confidence in your underwater offering.

One method that I have found successful is the "graphing" approach I use in every pool I fish. Mentally I lay a sheet of graph paper, or quadrants, on the surface of the pool, using slicks, underwater boulders or other visible permanent signs to mark each quadrant or square as I fish my fly. Because steelhead are large fish, when they are hooked they will remain where they are long enough for you to memorize their exact lie. In old English terms, this is a "holt," a location which will repeatedly produce fish. I cannot emphasize too strongly the importance of the holt! This is the precise location, the precise quadrant you hunt for when you fly-fish for steelhead! Once you have an experience repertoire of these specific locations, it becomes easier and easier to find these holding places in every new pool that you fly-fish.

Knowing that these homing steelhead are resting and not feeding fish, I will begin my casting dissection of the pool by first starting literally at my feet with short but controlled casts. I emphasize controlled because I have been astounded at the shallow depths some steelhead prefer, particularly if there is any run-off color in the water. Do cover the shallow white water at the head of a pool or run; steelhead like to rest in these specific areas.

As I move down parallel with the pool, constantly searching for underwater rock slicks which will vary considerably with the daily changes in height of the water flow, I will lengthen my cast to cover every location. I prefer a dead drift for my fly when I work these faster water areas of pools. I cast the traditional forty-five degrees upstream, mend my line and then wait for the ever so sensitive "tic" that tells me a fish has taken. But, most strikes with this style of wet fly-fishing are dramatic! As a steelhead takes the fly, the line will suddenly stop in your hand as the hook is set in the fish's mouth by the speed of the current pushing against the crescent loop of the fly line. You have a split second to memorize the lie and clear your line before the fish explodes in that magic fury that we associate with these trophy trout.

"Let him run!" "Let him run!" How often have you used or heard this call when a good fish is hooked? This is the most commonly voiced advice heard on the water when fishermen hook big fish!

Heed this call! It is the secret to landing steelhead! If you are fly-fishing for these fish you should have at least 200 meters of backing attached to your thirty-five meters of fly line. That is a long, long distance, almost a one quarter of a kilometer. Measure that one day in your car. You will be astounded at how far it is! Let them run!

One skill to be mastered by all fly-fishers hooking steelhead is the use of the reel to fight these big fish. I have often heard it said that in trout fishing the reel is really a carrier, a holder of the fly line. It is rarely used except when a lunker trout is hooked. With steelhead, however, every fish is a lunker! The only way to be consistently successful beaching these trophies is to master the use of your fly reel.

This summer I watched a frustrated fly-fisherman hook and lose a number of scrappy powerful steelhead before he clued to the hand coil system with his retrieved fly line. The system of coiling the line in your retrieving hand after so many strip retrieves does keep the line clear of the river, yet allows for free running fly line back through the guides on a hooked fish. This is one skill which should be practiced regularly because it is useful in a number of circumstances. To master this, establish a personal system where, after so many strip retrieves, say ten, loop the loose retrieved line in your stripping hand, then begin to strip retrieve once again. You will likely find that you end up with at least six long loops when you are ready to lift the fly and cast again. Use a power cast this time, releasing the loops one at a time as they are pulled from your hand. You will be surprised at the extra distance you are able to achieve.

Large fish take a long time to bring to the beach! Conventional steelhead rods all have a long butt which most anglers use quite efficiently to fight a fish. They lift the rod to bring in the fish, then lower the rod and reel in slack line. This is not possible, however, if you are using a conventional fly rod which has the reel seat placed at the extreme butt end. Sore wrists and lower arms are common and will, after a few lengthy fights, take much of the pleasure away from your fishing. A short fighting butt extension makes a considerable difference and gives much greater control of your reel over that powerful trophy. Some fly rods, in the larger weights, #8 and up, do come with these extension fighting butts. For those that don't, a quick trip to a local rod maker will soon have such a fighting butt constructed to perfectly match your favorite fly rod. I now have an extension fighting butt for all my large weight fly rods, many custom made and placed there by a friendly rod maker.

When casting, I keep the extension fighting butt in one of my fly vest pockets and shove or snap it on the rod as soon as I have a moment of control after I have hooked a fish. Try it. You will be amazed at how many more fish you will want to hook in a day's fishing and how much more pleasure you will get from those fish you are fighting.

We now know that the survival rate of fish released is often proportionate to the length of time spent fighting them in the river. At one time it was thought that salmon, who die after spawning, rarely survived if they were hooked and then released. This we now know is not true, in fact survival rates are usually quite high, more than 80 percent, providing the angler does a few survival techniques after the fish have been released. Never, never lift a big fish out of the water! Always wet your hand if you are going to handle the fish in any manner! Bring the fish to the beach as quickly as possible for a "hands-off" release!

Playing Big Fish—Some Quick Tips

Be certain that your backing is attached to your fly line with a smooth connection so that the knot will run smoothly through your guides.

Bow to every leap of these trophy fish. Their speed and height is certain to break your leader if you do not provide some slack.

Always keep your line tight to a fish when you are using a barbless hook. Remember these fish are continually working their jaws and one moment of slack will give them the leverage to spit out the hook.

Make your own leaders such that you are able to tie a new primary leader length after fighting each fish. A twist, kink, or fray almost always means a lost fish.

If there is one certain fact about winter steelhead, it is that they will rarely move from their resting location to strike at your fly. Knowing this behavioral trait is as important as the knot you use to tie your fly to your leader! This is the unique peculiarity of winter steelhead and it should dictate your presentation in every stretch of stream water that you fish.

Yes, there are major holding pools, which you know seem to always hold fish, but these are winter steelhead that you cannot reach with a cast fly! At two of these, on two Island rivers, I have spent years experimenting with casting techniques, weighted flies, and heavy grained fly lines. Every time I have drawn a blank and then, to add insult to my attempts, a partner, fishing with float and terminal tackle, has hooked a fish in the exact location I had been attempting to cover. Had this occurred only once or even twice, I would have considered that I had presented my fly poorly, but no, this has occurred many times over many attempts. Now, knowing that these situations occur, I tend to spend the majority of my time on more productive fly-fishing waters. Yes, I still experiment with these pools, but only when I have a specific new fly line or fly which I hope will overcome the difficulties facing me as a fly-fisherman in these waters.

If there is one area of a pool that I know produces fish, it is the tailout, that section of shallowing water at the outflow of the pool. This is magic steelhead water! Float-fishermen and drift-fishermen all have difficulty with these most productive sections of every river, but not so the fly-fisherman. These are the areas which hold well over 50 percent of all steelhead in a river at any given time. Mastery of these stretches will guarantee an increase in your "fish-on."

Steelhead prefer tailouts for a number of reasons. First and likely paramount is the fact that the river flow is constant, stroking both sides of the fish equally and in a comforting manner. Pools, on the other hand, tend to have alternating currents, vying with each other and moving and shifting any object, like a fish which tries to hold in one location. Feeling this, the steelhead will drift back downstream until the current has that single purpose and secure flow. The tailout also offers the greatest safety, for the steelhead, sensing any danger, can bolt downstream or dash into the depths which the pool provides. Other considerations are also involved in this tailout preference which seem to factor on the amount of light filtering down to the fish: these include water clarity, daylight/night, and cloud cover.

My most productive fly-fishing method for the tailout sections of pools is to use the "dead drift" method with my fly. This is the most common method used to sink your fly down to the depth at which a steelhead will be holding.

To accomplish this, wade out in the stream, cast upriver, almost into the main pool, then mend your line, and slowly strip line in to keep contact with the fly. By casting upriver, your fly will land in the calmer pool water which usually has minimum surface currents to belly your line. By the time the fly has reached the productive tailout section it is drifting just above the gravel and rocks, right where the steelhead rests!

I find that I will cast many times upstream, often far beyond the traditional forty-five degree angle, occasionally straight upstream concentrating on water between eighty and seventy degrees from where I stand. I know that I can wade and stand almost directly behind a fish before it is aware that I am in the stream.

Many methods are possible to get your fly down to fish in the faster waters of the tailouts of pools. Weighting flies are the most common and, once you have confidence in a pattern, you can tie this fly with varying weights for changing water conditions. I will usually use three different weights (wrappings of lead wire) on those patterns that I find most effective. These wraps, five, ten, and fifteen times around my hook, prior to tying my fly usually cover all water conditions; from the slow pool entrance to the tailout; to the faster midtailout section; to the rapids at the end of the tailout. Should additional weight be required, small spit shots attached to your leader usually suffice. I have found that using any more than three spit shots drastically affects my casting.

The tailout is that magic steelhead water! Concentrate your fly-fishing time in these areas of the river and I know that you will dramatically increase the number of winter steelhead that you hook.

More often than not, steelhead have that frustrating habit of first testing the pool where they are caught and then deciding to run-out! What can you do? I have tried many things, often in the wrong sequence, but, with experience, I have successfully beached enough fish to know that there are some tips that work.

When you first hook a steelhead make a point to *get the fish to the reel* as quickly as possible! Hand line fighting a large river fish like a steelhead is virtually impossible simply because your reaction time is always one split second behind the struggle, the head shake, or the run of the fish. The result is a snapped leader or a fly line tangle with a beach twig or some other flotsam debris.

Once you are "at-the-reel," *walk upstream* so you can hold the fish in the pool! The first reaction of the steelhead is to run from the pulling line. If he has not been stung by the hook, this usually involves a quick dash into the pool, followed by a downstream run. If you can keep him away from the tailout you can usually hold him in the pool.

Should your fish bolt out of the pool and reach the fast current of the tailout you must adopt a totally different fighting strategy. Give the fish line! Yes, even strip out extra line to stop the fish from dashing further downstream. Once the fish stops, *walk the fish upstream*. Do not reel! The jerking motion while you reel will start another downstream run. When you "walk-a-fish" upstream, keep the line tight and your rod still as it points straight out in the river, then simply walk upstream pulling the fish back into the pool. It works!

If the "walk-a-fish" technique doesn't work because the fish is too far into the tailout, you could have a partner go downstream below the fish and spook it back into the pool by slapping the water with a stick. Likely, however, the fish will not sulk long in the fast water of the tailout and will drift downriver stopping periodically behind larger boulders in the main current. If you are fortunate, the next pool will be on the same side of the river and you can simply run-slip-slide downriver as fast as you can, reeling in slack fly line as you go, until you are downstream of the fish. Unfortunately, on Island rivers it is rare to have two pools on the same side of the river due to white water hydrology and stream topography! The result is you must cross the river and get downstream of your fish if you are to beach that trophy!

Wading the river while fighting a steelhead is an art in itself! I have yet to meet the angler that can conduct this tricky operation all the while exuding confidence and skill! No, there is no smooth way to do this. Remember, your safety must be the first consideration! It is better that you break off a wildly running steelhead than to take a chance of injuring yourself or worse.

When I am faced with this situation, and my partner is with me, I always let him map out the crossing, guiding me downstream and across the river. I will have him hold me with a strong right hand on my jacket and walk upstream so that he takes the full force of the current against his legs. This way I am free to concentrate on a safe crossing and, at the same time, play my fish, keeping the line clear of protruding boulders, logs or undercut snags.

One of the most common problems facing anglers when they are dealing with a run-out fish is that of forcing the fish to the surface. This occurs when you tightly palm the fly reel hoping to brake the fish before it runs out of the pool. Never, never play a steelhead on the surface! Water acts as a containment on your hook helping to keep it in the fish's mouth. Should the fish struggle with it's head on the surface, the hook, in the air, will quickly snap back and forth, eventually pulling loose. As well, the power of the head shake quickly snaps any leader that does not have a cushion of water to protect it.

Fishing with a fly for steelhead in coastal streams is a challenge which only the fly-fisher can appreciate. Without question, other tackle is infinitely more effective for these non-feeding fish. But, for the converted fly-fisher there is an appeal with this tackle that defies explanation and which culminates in a personal euphoria when a fish strikes. It is that which is the nectar of fly-fishing!

Fly-fishing Equipment

The massive creel of fly lines on sporting goods supermarket shelves is enough to chase away anyone who wants to venture into fly-fishing for steelhead. "O for the good-old days of the single 'wet' line and 'dry' line!" was the comment of one of my angling friends last summer when he ventured into a sporting goods store to select a fly line for steelhead fly-fishing. I could well sympathize with him because, earlier that year, I had invested a considerable fortune in a number of new fly line "sets" for my more specialized salmon and steelhead fly-fishing.

If there has been one major advancement in fly-fishing in the past few years, since the introduction of graphite rods, it has been in the area of fly lines. Each year it seems that the various major name brand companies, Fenwick, Cortland & Scientific Anglers, are introducing newer and smoother materials producing more effective casting lines for the fly-fisher. The surge in recent fly line technology has given manufacturers the ability to create fly lines which can be used in any water, whether salt or fresh. This has allowed them to specialize in their production such that many now produce lines which target specific fish species, making it easier to select lines. This latter is evident in fly lines now called "steelhead," "trout," "bass," "bonefish," and "big game."

When considering a fly line for our large trophy steelhead, I would recommend the following:

1. Buy the best line(s) you can afford. Good lines will cost from forty to fifty dollars each.

2. Be clear about which specific situation you will be fly-fishing: summer or winter steelhead, large rivers or small streams.

3. Talk to a knowledgeable sporting goods store operator and ask that they explain in detail the lines they offer for sale so that you can select the one you feel is most suited to your fishing.

4. Focus on one line at a time and become proficient with it before you move to the next. Yes, it is important to realize that you will need more than one fly line.

5. *Only* purchase a fly line with a weight number matching your fly rod.

For steelhead fly-fishing, I would recommend the following fly line guide for these specific species and water situations. Note that each company uses a different name for their types of lines. I have generalized with the most common terms you should consider: for example, sink-tips, weight forward, floating and shooting heads.

Steelhead River Fly-fishing

1. Summer steelhead dry = weight forward, floating

2. Summer steelhead wet = weight forward, sink-tips (heads) of 5', 10', 20', 30'

3. Summer steelhead deep = shooting heads

4. Winter steelhead wet = weight forward, sink-tips (heads) of 10', 20', 30'

5. Winter steelhead deep = weight forward, sink-tips (heads) of 5', 10', 20', 30'; shooting heads

Now, having determined which steelheading experience you wish to pursue, select your line to match your fly rod. This is most important! Today, fly rods are built and assigned an international line weight number between one and fifteen, with one being the lightest and fifteen the heaviest. This is a standardized system adopted about twenty-five years ago by the American Fishing Tackle Manufacturers Association (AFTMA), now called the American Sportsfishing Association (ASA), and currently used by all name-brand manufacturers. Most fly lines are ninety feet in length. The ASA number is assigned to the first thirty feet of the line. This standardized system has greatly simplified the task of the fly-fisher searching for that "perfect" line match for his favorite rod.

For steelhead fly-fishing I would recommend a rod weight of #7, #8 or #9. Anything heavier puts too much stress on the casting arm during a day's outing, anything lighter has difficulty holding these large fish. For sporting pleasure, and to reduce the strain a powerful

45

fish will put in your wrist, a detachable "fighting butt" should also be a part of the rod you purchase.

Some Fly Line Tips

- When you select a rod and matching line, remember to consider the amount of daily use you will have for that unit. The #8 and #9 weights are power weights, usually involving a heavy four-ounce rod and a large spooling reel. Can you cast that kind of outfit all day?

- Rod length is a personal preference. I like a 9.9-or 10-foot rod for open-casting situations because of my tall height and extra arm length which gives me a good reach and strong arm-wrist power. On the small streams however, I prefer a 9-foot rod because of branches interfering with my backcast.

- Clean your lines on a regular basis using only mild soap and a soft clean cloth.

- Be careful to spool your new line without twisting it.

- Master the nail knot for attaching your leader to your fly line.

- Use the blood knot for attaching leader materials to each other.

- When using weighted flies on the riverbank beware of backcast fly tics on beach rocks. It is amazing how often the hook will lose it's point as it hits beach areas on the backcast.

"Is there an all-purpose fly line for steelhead fly-fishing?"

I have had this question asked of me many times and have always answered with a quiet, "No." "But," I have continued, "the closest line would have to be the sink tip (head)!"

The majority of steelhead river-fishing is done in deeper water where it is imperative that the fly be presented in front of the fish. The sink-tip (head) line presents your fly at the strike depth in the majority of cases or can be modified with weighted flies to obtain this depth under most circumstances. Because the back section of the line is a floating line it is easy to cast, retrieve, and mend—yes, the almost perfect line.

October, how I love this month! It is the time of the year when Island rivers are choked with salmon, when sharp clear days beckon the fly-fisherman to test his mettle in numberless streams. This is the month of autumn's low, clear water in coastal streams, waters which betray the presence of schools of magnificent salmon and steelhead. It is a glorious month, a month which makes these trophies visually accessible for perfecting fly angling skills and techniques. It is the one month of the year which, as a fly-fisher, I have learned to cherish above all others!

October is that month which gives the fly angler the greatest opportunities and, fortunately for the pocketbook, fly-fishing equipment used for steelhead can also be used for river salmon!

When discussing steelhead and salmon fly-fishing opportunities equipment costs have been a repeated concern. From my personal experiences I have found that it is only with the flies used for each that there is a major difference. But, even then, I have found that many steelhead fly patterns can be interchangeable when fishing for some salmon species like pinks and sockeye.

When I began serious saltwater fly-fishing for salmon I had already purchased quality equipment which I had been using for summer and winter steelhead. Because of this, when first experimenting on the saltchuck, I found myself able to cast and retrieve my fly lines in a manner which I soon found required only slight modification to become effective for catching salmon.

The Versatile Fly Reel

There are many many fly reels on the market ranging in prices to fit all pocketbooks. Unlike trout fishing where the reel's primary purpose is to hold your fly line, the steelhead fly reel is the key fighting tool in your equipment. Regardless of fish size I always, always, reel in my slack fly line before I attempt to fight the fish. Once "at the reel" I feel I have some control over these large fish and I can let them run from the reel whenever they resist the fighting action of my rod. When you finally decide which reel make you will purchase be certain that: the reel is easily repairable; spare parts are readily available; it is easy to clean; additional spools are available; it can stand up to a fast-running, knuckle-dusting large steelhead. Good luck.

Dual Purpose Flies

As a rule of thumb, I use "Silver" patterns for salmon and

"Pink" attractor patterns for steelhead. But, if you were to look into any of my many fly boxes you would see that there is variety! How often, in many situations have I found that the unorthodox, unbelievable, undefinable, and unreasonable strange fly was the fly that took fish. It is for that reason that I carry a wide selection of patterns, from optics to lead eyes, from streamers to attractors, from dries to bombers, to ensure I have covered all situations. I strongly believe that one can never have too many flies!

As an experimenting fly tier, I do feel there are some similarities between salmon and steelhead flies. First, because you must get your fly down to the depth which the fish prefer, salmon at fifteen to thirty feet and steelhead at the bottom of the river pool, the majority of my wet flies are weighted. This is the only certain way of getting my fly to the depth where these trophies lie. Secondly, I use stainless steel hooks for the majority of my wet flies, Mustad 34007 or the long shank 34011. These hooks add weight to help get the fly down. Anyone who has tied a box of nonstainless steel hooks and looked in your box after a day on the chuck will understand why you use stainless steel—always!

While dual gear will solve the cost element in your fishing equipment, there will come the time when you find that each situation, each species, requires a particular set of equipment. This is but one lure to fly-fishing. Each year, it seems, I add at least one new rod, one new reel, and a number of fly lines to my repository of tackle. Each winter I spend hours inventing new patterns and tying the tried and proven. This is the grand appeal to fly-fishing, likely the reason why it is the fastest growing outdoor sport in North America.

Sinking Flies

How often I have watched my fly rolling on the surface in that white fast water that I like to fish for steelhead. When it appears, flashing just under the surface, I give myself a mental kick and, after the drift, reel in the fly line and go to my weighted fly box for another fly. After switching flies, I will cast upstream again and wait for the sliding underwater ticks vibrating up through the fly line that tell me that my fly is now in the right location in the stream, drifting just above the stream bed rocks where the steelhead like to lie.

I have discovered, over the years, that for winter and summer run steelhead it is absolutely necessary to carry a complete fly box with weighted flies! At one time, earlier in my coastal fly-fishing career, I felt some embarrassment that I required weighted flies, still holding to my Okanagan dry fly upbringing. But, reality and rational thinking have squelched those earlier moralistic feelings. I now recognize that spring and summer dry fly rainbows are not summer, fall, and winter deep water steelhead. And, while I still carry one fly box of nonweighted flies, I match these patterns with three or more boxes of various weighted flies of the same fly patterns.

There are numerous ways to weigh flies, the most common being placing split shot on your leader. But, be warned with these visual weights for I have never hooked a fish when my spit shot have slipped down the leader and rested against the eye of the hook, a very common occurrence. Also, be cautious for in Island streams where special fly-fishing regulations occur, weights of any kind are not permitted on your leader or fly line. The solution in these regulated areas is, of course, weighted flies.

Because I tie my own flies, I will wrap lead wire around my hook before tying a particular pattern. Lead wire comes in a variety of sizes (large, medium, and small or numbered, for example, .025 for small) and can be wrapped in wide coils to spread the weight throughout the body of the fly or wrapped in concentrated coils close to the bend or eye of the hook to provide a specific dipping action to the fly when it is fished. Lead should be placed on the hook prior to the laying of any material or thread. This way it will always be covered when you have completed tying your pattern.

I have found that heavy hooks, particularly the barbless stainless steel variety that I prefer, are heavy enough to sink my patterns. Dentist x-ray lead sheets cut in strips are an additional good source of weight particularly as they will lay flat when wrapped around your hook.

I became acquainted with the "Chic" fly last summer while fly-fishing the Campbell River for summer steelhead. This innovative method has a lead split shot crimped to the shank of the hook adjacent to the eye. The split shot is then dyed or painted before the fly is actually tied. Once completed, the fly sinks quickly and in this particular example allowed the visiting German angler to work deep fast-water pockets at the head of deep pools. He claimed it was an American invention and one used for deep water brown trout. Lead eyes of varying sizes are another method for weighing deep-fished flies. They can be attached both for and aft of the hook shank and, for salmon flies, you can paint large eyes on their surfaces.

Be warned when you decide to use weighted flies. I can't count the number of times I have been whacked on the back of my head by my weighted fly or the number of times I have hooked my hat or head. In a wind, weighted flies can be a decided danger!

The steelheader's vest is a magnificent treasure box. Every spring I take a day to clean my vest of the numerous accumulations of the season. These items include everything from specially attractive stones and pebbles I have found on beaches; floats I have found drifting in the river; hooks and lures I have spotted in the river and retrieved; litter and fishing line I have collected from the riverbank; spare flies, pliers, scissors, lead, boxes, ziploc bags of all sizes, reel cases, surveyors marking tape, electricians tape to repair rods, glue and tape to repair wader leaks, and, last year, a doll I found floating down the river. Singularly, these items are of little consequence, but collectively, they weigh a ton! I am certain, like all steelheaders, there is no solution to the above except for the annual or, as I have found, at least a semiannual cleaning of my vest. One solution which has helped is the purchase of a second vest. I now have a special vest for winter steelhead fly-fishing only, as well as my vest for steelhead float-fishing. Will it help—only time will tell; perhaps I need another vest to carry the vests that I now have when I am combination fishing!

Three

Angling for Steelhead

The Strike!

The Strike!
The drifting float swirled with the merging currents,
Then fled with the foaming water,
Down to the tailout of the pool.

Again the cast,
Again the drift,
Again the race to the tail.
Again, and again, and again.

Then, it was gone!
Utterly, it disappeared!
A rock?
A branch?
A backeddy sucking it down in the murky green.

I pulled back on the rod to set the hook.
The solid resistance, unknowing,
An eternity of anticipation.
Then...the knowing shudder.

A strike!
A quick gathering of the slack
As the reel screams,
Its protest voluminous and full.

First, up the pool as always.
Then the panic;
The run down to leave the pool,
To escape!

This is the moment!
Can he be held?
Is he too big?
Is the knot tight?
Is the hook set?
Will he snag the line on a rock?
Will he break the leader?

He pooled!
He can be beached.

B. Thornton

The Steelheader's Language

In all specialized sports a highly selective language or jargon evolves. Steelheading is no exception! The following terms, commonly used by active steelheaders, will hopefully assist the novice angler in an understanding of this most addictive angling sport.

It should be remembered that many words have both a specific and a generalized meaning. For example, the term kelt colloquially refers to any steelhead in a dark condition, while in the scientific sense it refers specifically to any trout which has spawned. This term is often used in a derogatory manner to emphasize the unwritten ethical standard of steelheaders. The term kelt is used by steelheaders to debase any beached steelhead which is not silver and bright.

At first it might appear to be impossible for the beginner to distinguish fact from emotion, but experience and the Fishhawk will help to bring understanding.

Specific names are used to identify steelhead at various stages of their life, but, in the early stages, we use the common names applied to any *Salmonid*, or member of the trout and salmon family. These include the term "alevins" which defines the stage immediately following hatching from the egg when the yolk sac is still large and protruding from the stomach. When the young steelhead are free swimming they become fry and remain in the stream for periods from two to four years. When the fry begin their downstream migration during April, May, or June, they are called smolts. It is at this time that imprinting of the home stream occurs. After traveling thousands of miles in the open Pacific Ocean on their life odyssey, this imprinting will impel the adult steelhead to return to their specific natal stream and often to the specific pool of their early life.

Scale samples taken from adult fish are read as 2.2 fish or 2.3, 2.4, 3.2, 3.3, and 3.4, and others. These numbers refer to the life history of the fish. The first number counts the number of winters spent in fresh water while the second number counts the number of years spent in salt water. In most streams north of the fiftieth parallel of latitude steelhead have a three-or four-year stay in fresh water, while south of the fiftieth steelhead usually have a two-year freshwater stay.

Throughout their fry stage in fresh water, during winter periods, they will hibernate by digging deep, or graveling up, in river-bottom gravel. This gravel up process may also occur late in summer when water flows recede to ground water only for those fish living in small tributary creeks.

On their return from the sea as adult spawners, steelhead are called "green fish" because their scales are loose when they first enter fresh water. If they are still ocean bright, they are known as "chromers." At this time and until they become "dark" or "ripe fish," they are termed "clean."

On their upstream spawning migration the female steelhead, the doe or hen, does not alter her physical shape perceptibly. On the other hand, the male, the buck or cock steelhead, develops a large kype or upturned hook on its elongated lower jaw and a decided hump on his forward dorsal surface. Thus the male is easily distinguished from the female by an experienced steelheader.

Occasionally steelhead will return to their home river to spawn as "jacks." These are small male fish, often under a pound in weight, who have returned after only one year at sea. On the very rare occasion a "jill" will return as well. Half-pounders are also steelhead that return early to their home stream but, contrary to their name, they may actually weigh up to three pounds. The term is usually used in reference to small summer-run fish taken during the summer months or early fall, particularly in September. Scientists do recognize half-pounder populations in North America and Asia and specifically in certain river systems in southern Oregon and northern California. These fish are distinguished by unique behaviors in the marine migration phase of their life histories.

Kelts are fish that have spawned and are on their return trip to the ocean. They are often voracious feeders on their downstream trip and are occasionally referred to as "racehorses" for their habit of racing downstream non-stop on their initial run when hooked. Sadly, when they are caught by commercial salmon fishermen in the ocean they are called "snakes." This term is also used by steelheaders when they beach a long, thin, and narrow steelhead.

Steelhead anglers also use terms like chromer when they hook an exceptionally bright fish. Bigger steelhead, those over twelve pounds, have terms like "hogs" or "slabs" reserved for them, particularly if they are strong or aerial fighters.

Steelhead are classified as *anadromous* fish, meaning that they spend their early life in fresh water, migrate to sea for a major portion of their life then return to fresh water to spawn as adults.

Summer-run steelhead are a distinct race which enters streams from May through November on their spawning migration. Spawning, however, does not occur until the following March or April. Those summer-runs which enter the river late in the autumn are often referred to as fall fish. Although summer-runs can be identified by the thumb-sized seed roe in the body cavity, outwardly they cannot be distinguished from winter-run steelhead who enter their home streams from November through May. The main identifying feature is the time of the year when each enters the river.

The ardent and successful steelheader, often referred to as Fishhawk or riverrat, is a master angler on his home river, the stream where he will spend 60 percent, or more, of his angling time. If he is a member of the Steelhead Society of B.C., the organized provincial body of steelhead anglers, he is likely to be a stream guardian on his home river. As a stream guardian, his role will be that of a watchdog for environmental factors which may threaten the stream and a barometer of the feelings of other anglers and sportsmen.

The most likely disaster to threaten any stream is channelization of small or large portions of the river. This is known to destroy fish habitat in the immediate area and alter for years to come the stream bed downstream from the channelization. Many of the small tributaries to a stream will be ephemeral, meaning that they will dry up during certain periods of the year. Streambank logging, the clearcutting of all trees and vegetation without leaving a greenstrip, will result in flash floods downstream because of unchecked run-off waters. The steelheader, with anger and frustration at these common logging practices, refers to these as yo-yo streams.

For the steelheader, reading the water is a fine and intricate art. He will divide a possible holding pool, a specific location in the river where steelhead will pause and rest on their upstream migration, into three distinct areas. The head is the upstream portion of the pool

55

close to the shallows; the pool proper includes all deep sections from the head to the tailout; the tailout is the upsloping area immediately before the downstream rapids. Reading the pool, he will first look for a slick on the surface of the pool or tailout section. A slick will show as a smooth area of constant flow bordered on either side by roiling, uneven surface water. A slick is the desired holt or holding area of steelhead and is usually caused either by contrary currents meeting and balancing each other at that point or by an underwater object, a rock, ledge, stump, or tree trunk, which cuts the swirling currents and evens them out for a few meters.

Other areas in a stream also hold steelhead and these slots or runs are read to see if they have possible slicks which are holts or lies for steelhead. Walking-the-dog is a common technique used by experienced steelheaders to locate these hard to find steelhead runs. Here, the angler simply casts his lure out in the main current and lets the float drag it downstream with the main run of the current. Walking downstream parallel with his float, or, walking-the-dog as the expression has been coined, he will watch to see if the float bobs straight up indicating a deep depression where steelhead could hold. Often this technique is so successful on some streams which have their bottom gravel scoured during each high water flood that it becomes a standard angling method.

One-on! This is the booming cry of the successful steelheader when he has hooked a catchable steelhead. Anglers recognize that not every steelhead will take a lure or bait and it is for those that will, the catchable fish, that he hunts. On every trip he hopes that he will find a fresh run of fish, usually identified by their bright silver color and the presence of sea lice on the posterior lateral side near the vent. A run of steelhead usually occurs following a high tide when river water conditions are just right. The fortunate angler may find a small number of fish pocketed closely together or he may find a major run of many fish throughout the river, in which case he will have a bonanza expedition!

When a slick is identified, the steelheader will not shotgun a pool, that is, cast his lure out in any haphazard fashion. Rather, he will cast with skill, finesse, and care for he knows that if he has read the slick correctly and the depth accurately, a steelhead will usually take on the first drift through. Should his terminal tackle, the hook, lure or bait, weights and leader foul up, he will have another hook-up, previously prepared, ready to be tied on his main line immediately after he breaks off from the snag. Do not disturb the water and spook the fish! Should he roll-a-fish, that is, hook it but lose it when it rolls underwater showing a flash, he will rest the pool for some minutes before he again casts. If he is unsuccessful on his next drift he may feel that he has a spooky but catchable steelhead and will strip cast to the lie where the fish is holding by peeling line from his reel and casting free hand, holding the line like a fly line for greater control.

Most steelheaders detest a picket line, a group of anglers lined close together while they fish a known holding pool. Fishing for steelhead is a fine art and steelheaders would rather angle alone, free from the competition of other anglers.

Steelheading Truisms

All fishing and hunting sports have specific tips based upon the animal's inherited traits, the animal's habitat, and the sports specialized equipment which can be called truisms. Truisms in outdoor sports are reliable the greater percentage of the time and, if followed by the sportsman, are likely guarantees of regular success in his chosen sport.

Examples of truisms in other hunting and fishing pursuits would include: a buck mule deer's habit of pausing for a moment on the final ridge to look back at what disturbed him, before disappearing; the probability that a single bird will remain in the area where a covey of grouse has been flushed; and, the tendency of other trout or coho to circle a hooked fish and strike at another lure placed near the struggling fish.

Because of inherited traits, steelhead follow the same basic habits wherever they are found; these are the truisms of the sport of steelheading.

"Low Water—Fish High! High Water—Fish Low!"

Stream flows are the major factor in determining where winter steelhead will rest during their upstream migration as ripe fish or during their downstream migration as kelts. During periods of low flows the angler should fish at the head of the pool where the white water from upstream shallows provides a protective shelter for the fish. During high flows the tailout section of the pool provides the necessary conditions of flow, depth, light and shelter which the steelhead demands.

"Dirty Water—Fish Shallow! Clear Water—Fish Deep!"

Steelhead anglers agree that water color is an important factor and must be considered at all times when determining fish lies during fluctuating flows in streams. Heavy winter coastal rain and spring squalls color streams with silt and cause steelhead to move from major deep lies to shoreline pockets or very shallow tailout sections.

"Low Water—Light Line! High Water—Heavy Line!"

During periods of low flow, stream water is usually very clear resulting in steelhead which are highly selective and spooky. Thin, light, camouflaged line is absolutely essential for hooking steelhead under these conditions. During high flows, on the other hand, steelhead are less selective and more secure. Also, when hooked, they have a tendency to follow the faster currents downstream and can only be held with heavy line.

"On A Strike—*Memorize* That Exact Lie!"

When you hook a steelhead, memorize the exact location in the river where the strike occurred. This is a steelhead lie and it is the single most valuable experience fact that the steelheader will catalogue! A steelhead lie will remain in the *exact* (often within a few centimeters) location year after year unless the river changes from floods or stream development. The experienced steelheader concentrates on these lies during his day on the river, often traveling in haste from one to another, and then another, for he knows that it is from these lies that he will hook the majority of his fish.

"At Major Holding Pools—Fish Any Time Of The Day!"

Every stream has major resting locations where virtually every steelhead will hold on its upstream migration. Possibly these locations are genetically transmitted as a result of adaptation by a specific race of steelhead to the unique characteristics of an individual stream. These locations are the meat-holes of the river where anglers familiar with the stream will concentrate. River conditions may change from year to year and spring and fall floods may eliminate these pools. However, the serious angler can relocate these pools within a few hundred meters of their location in previous years. Since fresh fish are continually entering these pools, the angler can expect success at any time of the day.

"Fish The Bottom For Winter Steelhead—Always!"

There is a saying among steelheaders that angling expertise and the day's success will be judged by the number of lost terminal hook-ups! All steelheaders acknowledge that their terminal tackle must be drifting at the bottom of the stream if they are going to catch winter steelhead. On rare occasions a fish will take a lure near the surface. But, during a season, these times can be counted on one hand. They usually only happen when rain warms the surface water, when a voraciously feeding kelt is moving downstream, or when the angler comes upon an exceptionally catchable fish. Because steelheaders drift their tackle at the bottom where it is prone to catch on rocks or snags, they always carry terminal hook-ups prepared and ready for tie-up when their tackle is snagged or lost.

"Fish The Tailout!"

The tailout section of any pool is the area where steelhead prefer to rest. Tailouts provide constant and even flows of water and easy escape to the depths of the pool. The exact location of the specific tailout lie will vary with each pool and will be determined only after a fish is hooked. But, it is likely to be the spot where the main current flows evenly and creates a decided slick on the surface. My records show that the preference of steelhead is 60 to 70 percent for the tailout, 10 to 20 percent for the pool head and 20 percent for the rest of the pool.

"When Your Float Submerges—Strike!"

As simplistic as this truism sounds, it is the most common error of the inexperienced steelhead float-fisherman. An experienced steelheader can be recognized by the concentration he centers on his tackle while fishing. He knows that more than 90 percent of the time a submerged float means a snag or bottom. But, he will strike every time the float submerges for he knows that a steelhead will take in many unexpected ways and places and only when the float submerges will he hook a fish.

When float-fishing, the strike can be seriously affected if the line is not clear to the float at all times. This is the second most common error made by the inexperienced float-fisherman.

"When On The River—Fish!"

In general, it is not difficult to hook a steelhead once it has been located. The true skill in steelhead angling is locating your quarry. Steelhead angling in the Pacific Northwest is closer to hunting than any other form of fishing. Like the deer hunter stalking his prey, the steelheader also stalks his quarry.

It is amazing how many anglers will spend hours when they reach a river repairing tackle, tying hook-ups, and wasting precious fishing time! The successful angler anticipates the problems that he will face while on the river and will be equipped to deal with them in the least amount of time between casts.

"Confidence—Concentration!"

These are the hallmarks of the successful steelheader—the Fishhawk! These two traits obviously come from experience but they must also be earned. The novice steelheader should not expect any short cuts to the mastery of the skills and the confidence that distinguishes the Fishhawk. Only time, and more time, spent on the river mastering the intricacies of tackle, the habits and life history of the steelhead, the variabilities of the river in all seasons and weather conditions, and the secrets of reading water, earn the novice the name of steelheader. Concentration can come with a single season or even after a few trips with an experienced steelheader. But, confidence is the intangible that each individual will master only in his own time.

The Magic of Float-fishing

The cork float appeared to drag slightly as it drifted with the main current. One minute it was on the surface of the river, the next it was gone! I leaned back with the rod, reacting as quickly as I could to set the barbless hook. I felt the solid resistance of a hooked object, a slight give as it came towards me, then, saw the flash as it turned in the current and shot upstream! This was a good fish, chrome bright, obviously fresh in from the ocean.

The fish broke the surface once, twice, and then in a spectacular leap, shot high in the main pool, a good two meters in the air. Fortunately, his earlier leaps forewarned me and I bowed to this herculean effort of a classic west coast steelhead.

This was the second strike in that same location and, surprisingly, I found myself once again wanting more to cast and float drift then to play this prime three-kilogram steelhead. But the emotion passed as the hooked fish began a steady and rapid upstream swim, cruising past fallen logs and large boulders which were a characteristic of this pool. With churchilian determination, the fish entered the shallows at the head of the pool and continued swimming upstream in the fast water. His power was admirable, for, on reaching the shallow rapids of this smaller stream, his dorsal fin surfaced and I could see the tremendous power of his tail as he shot through the shallow fast water, striving for the next pool upstream.

I cinched up on my Hardy Silex single action reel, thumbing down as hard as I could without snapping the #10 leader. He paused, spurted forward again, paused once more, then turned and drifted downstream with the current. He was expended and came swiftly to the beach where I was standing. Close to shore I waded out and, with my needle-nose pliers, quickly released the barbless hook. Checking the main line and retying the hook, I cast another time to that most productive slot at the tailout of the pool.

The magic of the float, the story it tells, can only be compared to the rise of a trout to a dry fly. Like the dry fly, drifting with the current, steelhead float-fishing offers the appeal of the visual art of fishing! The float telegraphs messages to the angler which, when he has mastered their subtleties, creates a visual underwater picture of the action of his lure. It tells of small underwater currents by the slow rotation of the colored top; it tells of underwater rocks, large enough for steelhead to lie beside by the varying sixty to forty-five degree angles of the float; it tells of sand bottoms or gravel bottoms by the slow or jerky movement of the float as it drifts downstream. Every moment the float graphically displays to the angler what the bottom of each pool contains!

But, it is that ultimate vision which dominates the actions of the float-fishing steelheader, that moment when the float submerges! That is the moment that tells him that a steelhead has taken his lure! It is this latter experience for which steelheaders will concentrate for hours—unmindful of time, weather, partners, or spouses!

The experienced float-fishing steelheader can easily be recognized by the intensity of his stance when he has cast his float. Following his cast he is balanced on his toes, one foot in front of the other, ready for that instant step backward; arms are clear of his sides to ensure that no clothing will catch or hinder his strike; hands hold the rod high, up and away from his body; continually reeling or releasing line he keeps it clear of the water, clear to the float, ready for an instant strike should the float reveal a fish take. Once you have seen a master float-fisherman at work you can never forget the image or his intensity for that is what makes him successful.

In small coastal streams, it has been my experience that steelhead will take your lure on the first drift through the pool or run. For that reason it is important to be able to guesstimate the correct depth for that first drift. *Do not* overestimate! There is nothing more frustrating than hooking up on bottom and having to break off, often spooking fish in the pool with your line. Cast to the head of the pool with a short length between your lure and float and, on the drift, watch when the float suddenly drifts straight up and down. This is the drop off into the main pool and after lengthening your float you can cast to this area, using the same process as above to adjust your depth so that your lure bounces along the bottom. This drop off is one of the primary holding areas for steelhead and should be fished so that your lure bounces down the fast water at the head and drops down over the lip of the drop off and into the slower current below.

Once the terminal tackle has settled in the river, the float should point downstream with a forty-five degree angle if the lure is bouncing along the bottom. This is the correct angle for 90 percent of float-fishing drifts. It means that the lure is bouncing or dragging along the bottom of the river where steelhead lie.

Should the downstream angle be greater than this forty-five degrees, it usually indicates that your weights are also dragging on the bottom and if you are fishing a rocky bottom they will likely catch between rocks. However, if the bottom is sand, this drag technique can be used to slow your drift giving steelhead a greater opportunity to choose your lure.

When you first reach a steelhead pool plan your casts in such a manner that you are literally dissecting the whole pool. Consider the three main areas, the head, the pool, and the tailout. Start with the head of the pool and begin your cast so you are mathematically and methodically drifting your lure from the closest water to the water farthest from you. These drifts should be parallel to each other so that you are certain not to have missed any holding water. It is amazing how a single rock will alter the underwater current in such a manner to provide a specific holt, unseen on the surface slicks, where steelhead will lie.

Move downstream and, after lengthening your float, start to once again mathematically dissect the pool. You should start with a drift close to you and then drift your lure further and further out and away to the other side. Interestingly, steelhead will often lie in the shallows near each side at this deeper part of the pool, although, they will as often lie in the deepest water available in the pool.

It is difficult to determine, but every pool has one major holding slot where fish will lie. Locating this slot is the "hunting" aspect of steelheading! Once it has been located, it is fair to say that this will be the holding slot for the remainder of that year. Often, providing there have been no major floods, this holt will remain for years. The steelheader searches for these holts each season. Once he has found them he will likely use the 20/80 rule, that is he will spend 20 percent of his time to catch 80 percent of his fish concentrating on these holts. The remaining 80 percent of his time will be used to hunt for further holts for future fishing.

When you have finished drifting the main pool, move downstream and drift the tailout, watch it, this is where more than 60 percent of all steelhead are hooked! Why steelhead prefer this particular part of every pool is difficult to determine, but we do know that it is the result of the light factor in the shallower water and the specific current flow.

It is at the tailout that I allow my float to drag beyond the forty-five degree angle. This will slow the speed of my lure along the bottom giving the steelhead a greater opportunity to make the decision to strike. Yes, it does mean more snags, but I believe a successful day float-fishing is usually determined by the number of times you have hooked bottom; this is the knowledge that you have been fishing at the depth where the steelhead hold!

Rarely does a winter steelhead dash out, grab your lure, and streak back to his holding area. It does happen with kelts on occasion, and with a few summer-run fish, but it is certainly the exception! Most steelhead strikes are simply a mouthing of your lure which happens to be passing where the fish is holding. At the tailout of the pool any trick that you can use to slow your lure, making it easy for a fish to take, will give more strikes.

It is the terminal tackle which is the business end of float-fishing. Four main types of lures are used: bait hook-ups, soft latex lures, fluorescent wools, and hard-bodied lures like the Spin-and-Glo and Corkies. These should be tied at the end of a limp leader, lighter than your mainline, and should be about a third of a meter in length. The other end of this leader is tied to a swivel attached to your mainline. Weights, whether split shot or eared sinkers, should then be attached to the mainline immediately above the swivel and be set between five and ten centimeters apart. My preference is for the reusable split shot so that I can add or take away split shot to effectively drift my lure in fast or slow river currents. The ability of your float to just "cork" on the surface is often another effective tool. If the slightest pull will submerge your float, steelhead will often hold your lure for that additional split second which will ensure a successful strike.

The real success in steelhead float-fishing is to get your lure down to the fish. To do this, you must be constantly changing the depth of your float. If the float is continually submerging as you drift, you are dragging on the bottom and need to shorten the distance from float to terminal tackle until you have the forty-five degree angle. If you are not deep enough, the float will lie straight up and down. Lengthen it until you get the desired angle.

On more subtle takes, the float usually hesitates momentarily through the drift or dips slightly underwater. The fish may have taken the lure but, because of undercurrents, it doesn't register immediately or dramatically on the float. Or, as will happen, the fish may have risen from the bottom to the lure but only mouthed then released it. Persist in your casts through this section and if you are unsuccessful, lengthen your float a few centimeters to put it down to the fish.

Occasionally, in the larger rivers, you will find a pool that is too deep for normal float-fishing. One solution is to have a float with a very small hole—just large enough to thread your mainline through. At the desired distance along your mainline, say five meters, tie a small piece of thread that will hold firmly onto your mainline but which can be slipped up or down. On the cast, the float sits near your weights allowing for an easy cast. When the tackle strikes the water, the lure and weights sink to the desired depth while the float slides up the mainline to stop at the thread. Some anglers use a small bead rather than thread.

The following are some basic rules for float-fishing which hopefully will increase the number of strikes you will get. But, to play these magnificent trophy trout, that is your challenge! Good luck!

Float-fishing Rules

1. *Strike* immediately when your float submerges under *any* conditions! It is uncanny how steelhead will hold in apparent unholdable locations. Regardless of whether the water is deep or shallow, strike if the float submerges!

2. *Strike* at any unnatural float movement. Should your float show any movement which could be interpreted as a subtle take from a steelhead—strike! If you do not hit a fish on a strike concentrate on that specific site drifting your float in the *exact* location a number of times.

3. On every pool, change your terminal tackle depth at least three or more times by lengthening or shortening the float on the mainline. Locating those elusive steelhead holts is a true hunting skill which the steelheader must master. Your float action is a mirror of the river bottom and must be your eyes for underwater clues.

4. The variety of floats available today provide the float-fisherman with types for every water condition. My personal preference is for those built from cork or balsam and formed in the traditional torpedo shape.

5. Mainline should be at least a kilogram in strength stronger than your leader. I prefer the new fluorescent yellow, orange, and green lines produced by major companies to give me an uncluttered view at all times of where my mainline is located.

6. Dissect each pool with your casts. Start from the near side of the river and drift your float in parallel drifts until you have covered all possible holding water.

7. Use the line belly to strike sideways when the float goes under on those long drifts. While your mainline should be clear to your float in most situations, there are circumstances, like long drifts or long casts, where this is not always possible. At these times, a line belly is an effective strike tool when steelhead take your lure.

8. A good float-fisherman can be judged by the number of leader hook-ups he has lost in a day's fishing. How many did you lose today?

9. Rod lengths for float-fishing should be at least three meters to ensure that you can keep your line clear, at all times, to the top of the drifting float.

10. Winter steelhead are not feeding trout. Once you have had success with a particular lure, concentrate on that lure in all future fishing until you have confidence in your tackle.

If there were to be an epitaph for the steelheading float-fisherman, it would have these absolutes and, likely, it would read as follows:

Herein lies a Steelheader;
His eternal soul stands
Beside a celestial steelhead stream.
He holds an ethereal rocking stance,
One foot balanced in front of the other.
His float drifts in perpetual currents,
Forever pointing downstream at that angle,
Perfect, to ensure the seductive lure
Will bounce enticingly on ghostly river bottoms.
His oaken arms billow from his side,
His fishing rod is held high,
Locked in weather-worn hands,
The misty line forever clear to the float.
His eyes, ever red, so intent they never close,
For he fears he will miss that subtle float take
Of one more immortal steelhead.

Barry Thornton

Tips For Steelheaders

One on! One on! This is the cry of the successful steelheader. It is a booming sound of triumph and elation, muffled by the rushing water of a clear coastal stream, but still spine tingling as it floats on the elements of a coastal day. To the initiated it means a rapid retrieve, for who knows what may suddenly appear around the upstream bend where the cry rang out? When the auspicious cry sounds, there is less than a fifty-fifty chance that the fish will be beached—such is the power of the magnificent steelhead trout. But, if finally beached, the angler stands in awe at the size, the tenacity and the rare beauty of this fighting trophy.

Every month is the steelheader's month on Vancouver Island, with summer and winter steelhead available throughout the Island in more than 150 steelhead streams. The following steelheading tips have been accumulated from personal experience and from a continual reference to resource people, biologists and other steelhead anglers. Singularly, they may be of little significance and they are probably well known to many experienced steelheaders. Collectively, however, the knowledge from these tips could save years of frustration for the steelhead angler.

- In very clear water it is possible for the angler to watch the strike of a steelhead. Experience will show him that with bait, a steelhead will often rise to the bait and then drift slowly downstream with the current while he tastes the offering. This does happen in cloudier water and the float-fishing angler must be prepared on all drifts for the slight nudge of this subtle strike. With spinners and lures, on the other hand, the opposite is generally true. Most steelhead will hit a lure solidly and turn just as the lure is taken. The result is a pronounced strike!

- Unlike trout, which are active only during feeding times, steelhead will take bait and lures any time of the day. Steelheaders are on the river at daybreak only to be first on a pool. They recognize that there are only so many catchable steelhead in the river and they are available on a first come basis.

- Use one lure constantly, learning to fish it effectively and under all water conditions! Don't be mislead by the glitter at a sporting goods store, for experimentation will only destroy the sense of confidence that is a must for successful steelheading. Start with the recognized and successful lures, the Gooey-bob, the Spin-and-Glo, and the roe hook-up.

- While on the river fishing, check your equipment often and thoroughly. Retie knots, throw away frayed or nicked line and sharpen your hooks.

- A decaying log, lying diagonally on the beach, or with a portion in the river, points towards a steelhead lie! While this tip is not infallible, its uncanny accuracy has proven itself too many times to be ignored.

- Heavily overgrown stream sides often present hazards for casting. The experienced steelheader will quickly master the strip cast, where he holds loose line in his mouth or in coils in his free hand. This technique allows him to work steelhead lies in overgrown sections which under normal casting conditions are impossible to reach. Not surprisingly, many steelheaders prefer to strip cast in smaller streams once the skill is mastered because it gives immediate control of terminal tackle.

- Water conditions are the major factor for successful bonanza steelheading. Be certain to be on your stream immediately following a storm when the river has just started to clear and drop. Steelhead will normally move into streams in large runs at this time.

- If a steelhead shows interest in your float during warm spring weather by rising behind it, he likely will not take your drifted lure or bait. To hook this fish, take off your float and tie on a brightly colored lure. Cast this terminal tackle across the pool so that on a rapid surface retrieve it will cross the area where the steelhead showed on the surface. Be prepared! This fish will likely strike hard.

- Be certain that while you travel from pool to pool you drift your tackle through every section of dark water, regardless of how small it may seem. In clear water, deeper areas show a dark green and should be catalogued for high water fishing since they are probable steelhead lies. Some traveling steelhead are always scattered throughout a river and may rest in that particular small slick just behind a boulder that you are passing.

- West coast winters demand warm clothes and waterproof gear for the ardent steelheader. Chest waders are the most important item in the steelheader's gear and should be selected with considerable care. A pool can be fished properly from only one side. Chest waders are mandatory so that the angler can scout every pool and then, if necessary, wade across the stream to fish it from the correct side. A small patching kit or tape should be carried on every trip to cover the small punctures which will inevitably occur. Modern neoprene waders, while expensive, do provide flexibility, a must for riverbank hiking. I would recommend a lighter pair for those warm summer days. Felt soles should be glued on the soles of the shoes to give greater traction on slippery rocks, particularly in the spring months when the algae bloom occurs on river rocks.

- Unless you have absolutely no alternative, do not gaff or net a steelhead you choose to kill but, rather, beach it with your foot or tail it up on the beach. The only safe way to beach a large and powerful fish like a steelhead is to play him out completely, then slide him on his side up the beach. When he is in shallow water this can be done by guiding him with your foot or by clamping a hand around the wrist of his tail and gliding him on shore. Never beach a fish you are going to release!

- Never lift a large fish like a steelhead by the gills if it is to be released. Also, do not hold the fish up as the pull of gravity will injure internal organs. Remember that in most areas wild steelhead, those with their adipose fin, must be released. Do not beach these fish! Rather, while they are still suspended in the water, carefully unhook them with a pair of needle-nose pliers.

- Do not fish one pool too long. If you are casting and presenting your terminal tackle correctly, that is at the right depth and with

71

pool dissecting casts, a steelhead will usually take on the first few drifts.

- Always fish each pool in some pattern. Fish the head, the main pool, and the tailout as three specific areas. At each area start fishing close to you and then fish across the area in as many drifts as necessary until you have fished to the other side. It is only by using a pattern that you will be confident that you have covered all the lies in the pool. Fishing in this manner also enables you to fight a hooked fish in the area that you have already covered without spooking other fish you have yet to discover.

- While farther rivers always sound fishier, the novice steelhead angler should pick locally known and proven steelhead streams the first year and concentrate on those throughout that season. Fishy rumors are most often a case of "You should have been here last weekend!"

- Should a hooked fish run out of a pool and downstream past a seemingly impossible shoreline barrier, there is one trick that often works. First, strip extra line from your reel to stop the fish. Then attach a large float to your line. Next, cut your line and tie a swivel at the end so that the large float does not slide off in the current. Throw the float out into the stream and follow it downstream. When you are past the barrier, cast across the line near the drifting float. Retrieve the line and retie it to your mainline. The fight goes on!

- Lunker steelhead, those trophies that reach the twenty-to thirty-pound class, are not common in Vancouver Island streams. This is not to say that they are not available, for almost every Island stream will report a few of these fish every year. It is a fact that the longer steelhead stay at sea before spawning the larger they become. It was felt at one time that the largest were those that returned to spawn a second and third time. However, it is now recognized that while these repeat spawners may be large steelhead because they have spent additional years at sea, they are not the true lunkers for which the steelheader searches. Rather, the lunker steelhead are those that are slower to sexually mature at sea, taking three, four, and even five years, instead of the usual two years, before they return to their home river to spawn for the first time.

- Unlike the six Pacific salmon species, steelhead trout do not die after spawning. Physiologically they are able to reverse the deterioration that occurs following the spawning act and return to sea. Steelhead can return to spawn in fresh water a second, third, and even a fourth time. However, the survival rate for repeat spawners is not high. Depending on the stream, only 5 to 25 percent return to spawn a second time.

- The ratio of male to female steelhead returning to spawn for the first time is very close to one male to two females. However, the ratio of males to females returning to spawn a second time is one male to five females. This is a certain indication that females are much more capable of surviving the trauma of spawning.

- Stream size does not dictate the size of steelhead returning to spawn. Rather, it is the food conditions in the ocean which determines size. It is not uncommon for an angler fishing one of the smaller creeks to hook a lunker steelhead weighing more than fifteen pounds.

- When beaching a steelhead which is to be released, considerable care must be taken to ensure that scales and the protective mucus covering are not damaged. Green steelhead, or fish fresh from the ocean, have very loose scales which are easily dislodged. They must be handled with extreme care! The greatest danger to migrating steelhead comes from a fresh-water fungus which attacks the skin, eventually weakening and killing the fish. This white fungus, readily visible on dead and dying salmon, infects only weak or torn skin areas that have lost their protective mucus slime or scales. Fish should rarely be taken from the water as their internal organ can rupture in the air without the support of water. They should never be handled with gloves or wool mitts for these will absorb the mucus. Fish scales will tighten to the skin of the adult steelhead the longer the fish stays in fresh water. It has been researched and found that an angler-released steelhead will fully recover and continue his migration after about twenty-four hours of rest.

- It has been my experience that not all steelhead are catchable fish. In fact, I would hypothesize that in the majority of streams, 30 percent or more of adult steelhead will not strike, regardless of the tackle that is presented. Because of either behavioral, environmental, or genetic factors, these fish are noncatchable and this should be considered as an important factor in the overall management of this species. This is one important area of study for a salmonid ecologist.

- The following rule of thumb will give the steelheader a very close estimate of the weight of the fish he has just caught. A thirty-inch fish will weigh ten pounds. Add one pound for every inch over thirty and subtract one pound for every inch under thirty. Error will begin below twenty-five inches and over thirty-six inches. Male steelhead over thirty inches usually develop a humped dorsal surface which will add increased weight.

- Except for the different entry time, summer steelhead differ from winter steelhead in very few ways. However, there are two differences which the angler can cater to for better success. Summer-run steelhead will often actively feed while they are in the river and they tend to pocket in canyon pools while they are waiting for the spring spawning period.

- Steelhead anglers have two ways to tell how long a steelhead has been in the river. The presence of sea lice on the ventral side near the vent are a certain sign of a fresh fish. Sea lice die and drop off steelhead after a maximum of forty-eight hours in fresh water. The second indicator is the pearly mauve rays fanning out to the tip of the tail from the base. These colors are the result of calcium buildup in salt water and are absorbed by the fish as it stays in fresh water.

- During the winter, young steelhead "gravel-up" by hiding under large rubble and boulders in the gravel on the bottom of the stream. Here they hibernate during the cold winter months. In dry summer periods the juveniles will pocket in pools and then gravel-up until higher flows occur.

- Imprinting of the home river occurs for steelhead at the smolting stage, the time when they migrate out of their river to the sea. On the spawning migration, adult steelhead will enter the stream where imprinting occurred and, in many cases, will return to the same section of the river and even to the exact pool where they imprinted. Evidence for this is the fact that marked hatchery smolts often return as adults to the stream area where they were liberated.

- May and June are critical months for the survival of steelhead for it is during this time that steelhead smolts migrate to sea and are exceptionally vulnerable to trout angling. These smolts range from four to fourteen inches and are the trout that adults and children catch in massive quantities during these two spring months. It is a fact that the larger the smolt, the greater will be its chance for survival when it reaches the sea. But, unfortunately, these larger smolts are the most desired by spring trout anglers.

- A look at the annual take of steelhead by anglers is enough to deter any beginner. Of those who buy a license, 50 percent catch no fish; 40 percent catch one to five fish per season; six percent catch six to ten fish; three percent catch eleven to twenty fish and only one percent catch twenty or more fish each year. However, don't despair, each year there are many novice steelheaders who catch twenty plus steelhead their first season.

In concluding this creel of tips, I have prepared a specific section for the novice steelheader. I feel the information supplied will help the beginner to quickly find those first steelhead and thereby provide the hook that will forever pull whenever that angler crosses an olive hued stream.

Steelheading for the Beginner

A beginning steelheader is often told that it may take as long as two years before he actually beaches his first steelhead. After he has had some experience he may average one fish every ten hours of on-river fishing time and he will be fortunate if he beaches one fish for every five he hooks.

Not a very bright picture for the novice who wishes to start steelheading. However, there are many times when even the Fishhawk will draw blanks and he may spend from three to five hours of on-river angling for every fish he beaches. The Fishhawk's constant success, however, is the result of three major factors.

First, he knows his river and he knows when the fresh runs usually arrive. This is an experience factor and usually only comes with time. River inventories by Department of Fisheries can hasten this knowledge, for most streams have been catalogued and then major run timing determined.

Second, they will always fish their terminal tackle where the steelhead lie—not a few centimeters or meters above or to either side of the fish, but in such a manner that whatever lure they are using will drift or pass directly in front of the fish.

Third, they take an almost fanatical care with knots, the placement of weights, and the adjustments necessary to make their terminal tackle perfect. They know from experience that a minutely frayed or crimped line or a poorly placed and tied knot means a lost steelhead when he explodes at the strike.

During his first year of steelheading the novice should concentrate on one of those smaller streams which are known to have good runs of steelhead. The selection of small streams is wide on Vancouver Island and includes such famous streams as the Big and Little Qualicum Rivers, the Quatse, the Keough, the Quinsam, Harris Creek and the Englishman River. Many of these streams have been augmented with hatchery steelhead and these add to the possibility of hooked fish.

Once the beginner has selected a stream, he should stay with that stream for the majority of his fishing time that first year. This is a must if the techniques of steelheading are to be learned in one season. It will often be difficult as the season progresses, particularly as bonanza runs in other Island streams are reported. But, be patient, watch other more successful steelheaders, talk to these individuals as often as possible and build your own repertoire of confidence in your skills.

The major advantage of the small stream for the novice is the concentration of all the factors necessary to become successful. The small stream miniaturizes all the conditions of the larger rivers and this knowledge is transferable.

Beginning steelheaders can be confident that when one stream runs hot with fish during the main season all other streams in that region will also be running hot with fresh runs. This may not be the case early in the season, but once the new year arrives this rule of thumb follows, providing weather conditions are similar.

Having decided upon a stream, the novice should fish during high and low water conditions and during freshets and colored water periods. This will include weathering storms, freezing temperatures, torrential downpours, and blasting winds. It will, as well, include shirt sleeve weather and times when the fish seem to be in every pool and your arm aches from the fight of a good fish.

While on this classroom river, master casting techniques and terminal hook-ups and then select two or three lures which you will continue to use during the whole season. The first year, the best selection would be: roe with red wool tied to the hook; a #12 pink Spin-and-Glo lure; and, an orange Gooey-bob covered with a thread of white fluorescent wool. Have a selection of these ready at all times and fish with nothing else.

The terminal tackle is the business end of your fishing gear and must be tied with dedicated concentration. The following are proven methods for tying your terminal tackle.

The hook-up for your terminal tackle will depend on whether you are float-fishing or drift-fishing. Both methods have many items in common but there are some basic differences.

Float anglers usually rig their terminal tackle in the following manner. At the end of their fifteen-to twenty-pound test mainline they will tie a #4 or #6 swivel. Tied at the other end of the swivel will be a leader of from ten-to fifteen-pound strength, always a few pounds less than the main line. The leader will be about forty centimeters long, ending at the hook. The hook will be an offset hook with an upturned eye in at least a 1/0 or 2/0 size. The hook will be tied to the leader with a clinch knot, if a lure is to be used, or a barrel knot tied on the shank of the hook to make a lasso for the bait.

Placed on the main line directly above the swivel will be sinkers of sufficient weight to take the lure down in the current. Sinkers are usually split shot or eared sinkers placed three to five centimeters apart above the swivel. Eared sinkers have the advantage for they can be taken off when necessary, while split shot placed on the line is permanent and often slips down the line jamming at the swivel. Eared sinkers are kept in place by first crimping one ear over the main line, then wrapping the main line around the sinker at least three times and then crimping the remaining ear over the main line.

Above the sinker is placed a float, preferably of the torpedo shape since this allows less drag when a fish takes the lure.

On Vancouver Island, drift-fishing is usually done on the larger sandy-bottomed rivers like the lower Campbell, the Salmon, the Stamp, and the Cowichan. While the lack of a float is the major difference in this type of fishing, also less tackle is lost if the weights used are different. Usually no weights are tied to the main line. Instead, a tri-swivel is used and to the third end is attached a very short leader which has a small strip of surgical tubing tied to it. Jammed into the open end of this rubber is a six-or eight-inch tube of pencil lead.

The drift fisherman casts upstream and then bounces the pencil lead along the bottom of the river in a wide arc waiting for the strike of a fish on his lure. Should the pencil lead become stuck, the angler merely pulls it out of its rubber fitting or breaks the light leader to save his terminal tackle. The float-fisherman, on the other hand, usually snags his hook but breaks the leader, saving his weights and float.

Many adventures await the beginning steelhead fisherman and I am envious of his opportunity to experience this early introduction to steelheading. In other chapters in the book I have detailed additional tips and concepts which will provide steelheading success. I wish the novice well and hope that I am one of those anglers he stops for a chat while he travels our magical waters.

Wading The River

Standing on the river trail, I watched the beaver noiselessly swim and drift downstream with the current. I silently prayed for the thousandth time for this friend of the steelheader. How many times, I asked myself, during many winter steelheading seasons have I watched their engineering progress on a fallen alder or evergreen tree that had effectively blocked a pool or shallow riffle. By gnawing until all branches were stripped or cut off, they released the trunk to drift downstream but up against the riverbank and cleared it from a steelhead lie. How many times, I thought as he disappeared downstream, had they chewed that solid third leg which had propelled me safely across uncountable rain swollen rapids? Yes, the beaver is a river friend of the steelheader. He ensures clear fishable streams, headwater nurseries, and supplies a solid light wading staff unmatched by any manufacturer or advertised in any catalogue.

Many years ago, I purchased one of those lightweight telescopic aluminum wading staffs only to find, when it was put to a severe test, one of the extensions would slip and throw me off balance. Once, I remember only too well, I fell head first into cold February river waters when an extension tube suddenly gave way, leaving me soaked many river bends from my truck. This reminder of our technical world still hangs on a peg at home but, now, it is almost hidden by the collection of beaver chewed lightweight wooden staffs that I have since collected along Island riverbanks.

River wading is one of the most important river skills steelhead fishermen need to master if they are to be consistently successful and enjoy a day's fishing. It is a skill which is mastered only after many years of experience but there are some tips which can hasten this mastery.

When you wish to cross a stream choose your crossing carefully! The easiest water is usually at the tailout of a stream pool. Here the main force of the current is slowed and the water depth is hip-deep or higher.

Drift with the current as you cross. Forcing yourself upstream will often undermine the sand and gravel underfoot resulting in treacherous unstable footing. I like to "cork" as I cross a stream, bending first into a crouched kneebend position and then I flow with the current to bob down and across the stream.

Always "crab-walk" when you wade! Keep your knees bent and crouch forward to give yourself complete balance as you move across the stream. I have found that high hip-or waist-deep water allows a buoyancy which gives much greater control and balance.

Often when I am crossing a new section of river I will wade into the stream until I am in waist-deep water. Then, following the contour of the pool, I will walk-bob-cork downstream along the near side of the stream until I have found the hip-deep contour at the tailout of the pool. Here is where I will then wade across to the far streambank.

Point your foot upstream when you are wading. This gives a much smaller surface for the water to bypass and at the same time it gives you a control over where each step can be placed.

Do not turn your back on the current! This is the position of least control! Once you have done this you will find yourself stumbling constantly, eventually to fall in the water.

Beware of river flotsam! Small twigs, bark, and branches are a certain sign that the water level is rising. When you see these in the river plan your crossings carefully so that on your return you are still able to wade back across the river.

The most dangerous water to cross is that which is ankle-or calf-deep rushing over cobble stones. The danger comes from the injury you might receive when you stumble and fall.

If you have a partner, cross with one hand tightly gripped on the shoulder of each other's coats. Holding onto shoulders gives both of you the freedom of an arm's length to step over boulders or other hidden underwater snags. When crossing with a partner, the upstream angler should use a wading staff with his free hand while the downstream angler carries the rods in his free hand. If you are crossing a particularly fast and forceful current, one angler should brace himself before the other moves forward; then, the other angler moves forward and braces himself; and so forth, until you have negotiated the treacherous section. Finally, when with a partner, don't release your hold until you are both on dry ground! It is amazing how often, in the last few feet before the bank or beach, you will stumble, fall, and injure yourself on rocks. Your partner's balance is most critical during these final few meters!

Wading can give the stream angler access to all parts of a stream often necessary to effectively cover a fishing pool. A wading staff, your third leg, should always be used! Felt soles and wading cleats are particularly effective and an investment that is a must for sound, safe, and secure river angling.

The following are "wading do's" which, if mastered, should lead to continued and pleasurable steelheading success!

Do—map out your crossing route carefully before wading into the stream. Always consider your return route in your mental map.

Do—use a wading staff at all times when crossing for it provides a third balance point. Don't let go of your wading staff until you are actually on dry ground on the other side; most dunkings occur on the far bank in shallow water when the angler feels he has safely navigated the deep water. If you are using a riverside branch as a staff, place it where it is easy to use on your return or for another angler to use.

Do—secure your wading staff ahead of you in fast water. Take small steps and make certain that your staff will hold on slippery bottoms.

Do—choose as your wading area the section of a pool just prior to the tailout where the water is thigh-deep. This is important for safety for, if you slip, you will drift to the shallow water at the tailout.

Do—choose water that is waist, thigh, or knee-high rather than ankle-deep water. Ankle-or calf-high water is usually faster and visibly more unbalancing.

Do—fish your pool thoroughly and close to shore before you step into the water.

Do—choose chest waders for steelheading, not hip waders. Chest waders should be loose enough to allow you to bend your knees to step over logs. If necessary buy one size larger and use insoles.

Do—use your rod for balance on the water, if necessary, laying it flat out on the surface. Tests have shown that it is highly unlikely the rod will be damaged for it will bend in its natural curvature on the stream surface.

Do—wade the stream together if you are fishing with a partner. His support will provide an extra balance point and often he will hold you upright if you slip. Wet your hand to get a nonslip grip on his jacket.

Do—drift with the current in a semi-crouch position. Keep your arms out like a tight rope walker for extra balance. Secure each foot before you transfer your weight. Keep your toes pointed upstream or down to expose the narrowest surface of your leg and ankle to the current.

Do—use a "floater," a government-approved safety type of coat, worn over your waders for safety and buoyancy. Be certain all clothes are buttoned or zipped prior to crossing and that you have clinched a belt around the top of your waders. It is surprising, if you follow the above, how little water will actually leak into your waders should you fall.

Do—observe the natural clues of the river when you are wading; dark green water means depth; floating debris and small sticks indicate the river is rising; a slick in midstream results from an obstacle instream; a stump in the stream is a sign of a deep hole where the river first meets the stump; sandy bottoms indicate slow water; rocks and heavy gravel indicate fast water.

Do—wade your favorite stream during periods of low water to find all the holes, lies, slicks, troughs, and bank undercuts where steelhead will rest when high water and freshets bring them into the stream.

A great deal of adventure and abundant success await the wading steelheader. However, caution, intuition and a strong wading staff should always be your partner and your guide!

Unique Steelhead Angling Experiences

Did you ever hook a steelhead through the top of the head or the tip of the tail? Would you believe the dorsal fin? Maybe you would believe lassoing a steelhead? No? How about hooking the pectoral or pelvic fin?

In conversation with some anglers on the riverbank I related some of those strange experiences that all anglers have. Mine dealt with steelhead and the odd places where I have hooked these fish and yet still managed to beach them. I know many anglers have had similar experiences and each is a tale in itself.

Probably my strangest was an experience on the Park Run of the Quinsam River. I had drifted the pool a number of times before the float made that tell-tale dip in the current that warned me a steelhead had taken my lure. I struck and was fast into what proved to be a bright fourteen-pound doe. After the initial spurt up and down the run I set myself for the dogged water-walking battle that usually follows. However, this one was different! She turned downstream and headed full steam for the Campbell River, about 1,000 meters away. I thumbed my Silex to brake her but had to ease the pressure when I felt it was at the breaking point. I then tried the next trick—stripping slack line to give her the impression that she was free, but again, to no avail. She was now at a bend fifty meters downstream. I had no choice but to charge out into the river and wade downstream after her.

The run was deep and as the water began to flow over my chest waders I bobbed up and down in the current, heading for the bank on the far side. All the while I kept snubbing the reel, forcing her to a surface thrashing fight. Surprisingly, she tired rapidly and allowed me to gather in the slack line and put her on the beach around the next bend. On the shallow rocks I spotted the hook, embedded, not in the mouth but on the top of the tail about an inch from the end!

Lassoing a steelhead has to be a fish tale that only a westerner could tell but, as I am on Vancouver Island...I had spent a day on the upper Big Qualicum with little success. Late in the afternoon, at the Trestle Pool, a few hundred yards upstream from the hatchery site, I half-heartedly cast my tackle into the pool. I was hoping that a fresh fish had arrived and escaped the countless anglers that usually fish that area. The float dipped and I struck. The reel screamed and a bright eight-pound steelhead showered spray all over the pool as he fought to toss my hook. The fish dove deep and fought doggedly for quite a span of time. Then I reeled him towards the shore. As the fish came close my partner suddenly leaped into the pool and reached for him. It dove—he grabbed! Sputtering from the near dunking, he laughingly hoisted the fish for me to see. The line was cinched in a lasso on the belly just behind the pectoral fins. It appeared that the hook had slipped out of the fish's mouth during the underwater twisting struggle but had caught on the mainline, making a loop which in turn had cinched around the fish's belly. Constant pressure on the line had kept the loop tight until the moment he was grabbed.

Steelhead striking the float rather than the bait has to be one of the most unnerving incidents in a steelhead angler's experiences. Waiting and intently watching for the tell-tale dip of the float is absolute concentration—but, to suddenly see a steelhead mouth appear gulping the float from underwater is nerve shattering. This unorthodox strike comes from the very active steelhead and all float-fishermen eventually experience this moment. But what if the float should get stuck in the fish's mouth? This happened to a friend of mine on the Salmon River. After the large fish struck his float he played it as if it were caught by a hook and beached a prime sixteen-pound doe. Checking the fish, he found the skewer stick of the float caught in the mouth wedged in the lower jaw. The fish could neither close or open its mouth after the float lodged there on the strike.

How does one hook a fish in the very top of the head? Even in my wildest speculations I cannot attach a set of circumstances to this situation. However, fishing the Trent River, I hooked a clean fish above a log jam only to have it take its initial run under the logs. The rod stayed solid for a long time and I believed that the fish had snagged it to a log. After a few minutes of frustration I wrapped the line around my wrist, pointed the rod tip at the log and backed away to break off. Suddenly, the line around my wrist tugged and tugged. In much confusion I got it unwound and soon had a pool-walking steelhead dancing in front of me. I played it carefully and soon eased it carefully on the rocks at the tail end of the pool. You can imagine my surprise when I spotted the hook firmly embedded in the thick tough skin at the very top of the head.

Combination fishing for steelhead appears to be another oddity. In all my years on steelhead rivers I have yet to see another angler follow the simple river rule of fishing with what is appropriate for each pool. I am amazed that steelheaders do not take two rod combinations with them when they do angle on steelhead streams. The following story, a common experience I have had, shows what occurred just one day and what is possible for the steelheader who will use the combination method.

It was late morning when I waded the shallow bar below the Caribou Run on the Oyster River. The freezing water from the late mountain run-off iced through my thin waders before I was halfway across. But, the warm day, the first real spring day, eased the chill after I was on the far bank.

Moving upstream parallel to the middle of the Caribou Run, I noted puddles of ice which the sun had still not reached and frost-crushed trillium leaves which were bowed in the shade of the willows and alders.

The river had been clear earlier in the morning but was beginning to milk from the melting run-off snow and ice. The clay-sandstone ledge on the far bank was under four or five inches of water, indicating a perfect angling flow. A dark break, visible underwater in the ledge and disappearing into the river gravel bottom, pointed directly to the steelhead holt where I have hooked so many good fish.

Combination fishing this day, I carried two rods. The first was my regular nine-foot Fenwick fly rod, line weight #12, which was perfectly balanced with a Hardy Silex reel for float-fishing the deep holes. The second was a nine-foot-nine-inch Fenwick fly rod, line weight #8, with sink-tip fly line which I used to cast to those ideal fly-fishing steelhead runs on the Oyster River.

April and early May are ideal months on Vancouver Island for combination angling. As the long winter steelhead season draws to an end, more and more steelheaders, satiated by their winter's success, bring out their fly rods hoping to lure a majestic steelhead with fly tackle. They realize that only a small percent of the steelhead lies can be covered with regular fly-fishing tackle but, having recent experiences on those waters, they will spend lengthy periods persisting with the fly lines. Only when they are certain that they have not touched a fish will they then work the run with the float rod tackle. They know that its deadly effectiveness is many times greater than fly casting.

The Caribou Run is one of those near perfect fly-fishing runs. A sloping gravel beach drops into a trough created by a steep bank on the far side, a common occurrence on smaller Island streams. Here the steelhead hold, moving up and down the trough depending upon water depth and clarity.

I tied a weighted rainbow patterned fly to the very short two-foot leader and began to send ever-lengthening casts out over the river, working slowly towards the water above the main steelhead lie. A swift current demanded a mend of the line each time the fly hit the water, but soon the rhythm and tranquillity of the pool mesmerized me.

Distance is not important when fly casting. When I had reached what I felt were tolerable limits for control on the pool, I compensated for any lack of distance by wading out into the current.

After every three casts, which covered the river upstream from where I was standing at the desired forty-five degree angle, I would sidestep three steps downstream and work the three patterned casts once again. Occasionally I felt a slight "tick" as the fly brushed against rocks on the river bottom. This was a certain sign that my fly was down on the river bottom where the fish held. All that was needed now was a solid strike from a steelhead.

A sudden halt in the drift broke the tranquillity and I automatically lifted the rod tip to set the hook. A moment of eternity passed as I waited, wondering if it was fish or snag! Then, a silver flash lit the river bottom and the line streamed through my fingers.

The first run took the fish to the tailrace of the pool where it catapulted in fury, throwing a showering rainbow spray. It took another short run into the downstream rapids and I felt the thin backing race through my fingers. But, there it halted and shook its head to test every weakness in that eight-pound test leader. Then, it bolted upstream as I frantically tried to reel in the slack. At the head of the Caribou Run it leapt once, twice, dived, then leapt again! Finally, it sounded to the river bottom where it drifted downstream until it lay in the main holt. There began the dogged, line-torturous fight so typical of steelhead. In one last gesture I could feel the nose butting on the river bottom as it tried vainly to dislodge the hook.

When finally I eased it on the beach the fight was completely gone. It was a startlingly beautiful hen, bright as tinsel and pushing nine pounds. My day was complete for I had earlier beached a small buck using a Gooey-bob in the deep pool immediately below the Caribou Run. Unlimbering the fly rod, I packed it together with two of the many elastic bands I always carry with me, my combination day a complete success.

Four

Some Vancouver Island Streams I Have Known

An Introduction to Vancouver Island Streams

While writing about steelhead, I have experienced a flood of memories about this elite of freshwater game fish, about specific adventures and about the river environment. But, of all these memories, the river environment has remained the most fixed in my mind, for the streams, with their stable headwater pools, their access points and their wildlife, have been my constant companions. Their consistency, as opposed to the elusive and unpredictable nature of the steelhead itself, has given me security and confidence in the sport.

I will be criticized for mentioning specific rivers, access points, and pools in this book. Some anglers hide their knowledge from novice steelheaders and even from managers but, unlike them, I believe that steelheading is a unique Pacific Northwest angling sport which must be shared if it is to be managed effectively and preserved for future generations. If we are to perpetuate the sport, the novice must have the confidence necessary to endure the average two year initiation and eleven hours of on-river angling time for each beached steelhead.

I do not fear for steelhead rivers if there is an article published on them. Rather, I feel that steelheaders are natural river guardians and publicity brings angling numbers to ensure the protection of our streams. Steelheading is site and time specific. Sharing knowledge of these rivers is the greatest guarantee we have that the resource and the river will be a gift we pass on to the next generation. Remember, the unknown river has no friends!

We can give confidence and even shorten the initiation period for the novice by providing guidance about "where" and "how." We can also provide information which will narrow the range of "when" but, ultimately, the novice steelheader must master that latter element alone by confronting the unpredictability of river flows and temperature and the river specific timing of steelhead runs. Here there are no short cuts, no secrets from books. Only river time will make the novice a steelheader!

Since the introduction of the federal provincial Salmonid Enhancement program in 1976, one of the most elusive factors, that of stream specific species information, has been overcome. But still, for the managers, one of the most frustrating aspects of stream specific management is the lack of accurate historic information including details of steelhead ethology in each stream and records of anglers' experiences. This information is available in the comprehensive diaries all steelheaders keep. The onus is on both steelheader and manager to maintain and share this information for future management. The managers must make the effort to retrieve this information and the steelheader must be prepared to relinquish his secrets.

Likely the greatest selection of steelhead streams on the east coast of Vancouver Island lies in the seventy-kilometer stretch of the Island Highway between Parksville and the Comox Valley. Variety is the byword for this area, with small creeks, large rivers, controlled river flows, yo-yo streams, lake fed streams, run off streams, late fish runs, early fish runs, drift-fishing, float-fishing, fly-fishing, winter steelhead, and summer steelhead.

The geographic formation of Mt. Arrowsmith, the sheer Beaufort mountain range, Mt. Washington and the Forbidden Plateau, knifing along Vancouver Island in this area, accounts for this variety. Beginning in the south, the vast southeast slope of Mt. Arrowsmith feeds the Englishman River. Pocketed between Mt. Arrowsmith and the Beaufort Range are Cameron and Horn Lakes, the reservoirs for the Qualicum Rivers. The high Forbidden Plateau and the mountains surrounding the Comox Glacier feed Comox Lake, the reservoir of the Puntledge River. The broad slopes of Mt. Washington, which rises over 1,700 meters, feed the unique runs of steelhead which enter the Browns and the Oyster rivers and provides the run-off for the Tsolum River and Black Creek.

Between these two imposing peaks, Mt. Washington and Mt. Arrowsmith, are a multitude of small creeks and streams, the result of heavy and rapid run-off from the linear slopes of the Beaufort Range. They tend to be "flashy" in the steelheader's jargon, providing excellent steelheading should the angler chance to hit a run of steelhead.

Two major rivers, eight streams, and seven notable creeks all cross the highway in this hour-and-a-half drive from Parksville through the Comox Valley. All are accessible from the Island Highway and most have side roads which provide additional upstream access.

Traveling north through this steelheader's mecca, the Englishman River crosses the Island Highway on the southern outskirts of Parksville. The Englishman provides early winter steelheading with fish runs entering the river early in December and continuing through to late April. In recent years, the Englishman has been heavily augmented with hatchery steelhead who, with the wild population, provide some outstanding steelheading. Access to the middle Englishman River is from Kay Road off the Island Highway or from side roads off the Alberni-Parksville Highway. Fly-fishing, float and drift-fishing are equally successful on this pleasurable angling stream.

Four kilometers north of Parksville, the Island Highway crosses French Creek, one of the more productive small creeks in this region. It has winter steelhead but is spotty. Runs have declined rapidly in the past decade. Access is from private farmlands, the highways, or off urban settlements.

Just north of Qualicum Beach the angler crosses the first of the Qualicum Rivers—the Little Qualicum. It is a high-quality angling stream which provides fly, float, and drift-fishing opportunities. It has been heavily enhanced with hatchery steelhead and provides outstanding steelheading from December through May. Lower river access is available from the Island Highway. Upstream access is from Montrose Road on the Alberni Highway.

Ten kilometers further north on the Island Highway is the Big Qualicum River with controlled flows and controlled temperatures. Controlled flow guarantees fishing regardless of weather conditions, a feature which has made this a popular destination for local steelheaders. Winter steelhead enter the river early in December but the mass of spawning chum salmon from this federally developed Department of Fisheries hatchery and project make it virtually unfishable until the new year. The steelhead run peaks late in February but many steelhead are caught well into May. Access is from the hatchery and then the fisheries road which parallels the river (hiking only) or from the Horn Lake Road. In recent years, instream structures have created fishable pools which are numbered. Greatest success can be had by float-fishing this small stream.

Between the Big Qualicum River and the Courtenay River lie Nile Creek, Cook Creek, Rosewall Creek, Cougar Creek, the Tsable River, Washer Creek and the Trent River. These small systems are float-fishing streams. Major access is from the Island Highway. Water conditions are the key factor for these systems and the angler must fish them either just as they are rising from heavy rains or run-off or, conversely, just when they start to recede. Winter steelhead are spotty, non-existent, or in surprising numbers, from December through April.

Once the streams feeding the Courtenay River provided world renowned steelheading from December through June. It is a sad state that the Puntledge River, the major river, has been closed because of the very few summer and winter steelhead that still remain. The Browns River, accessible from the Forbidden Plateau Road, has a very late run of winter steelhead in May. Sadly, the Tsolum, the second major tributary, has been poisoned and it may be years before this river again provides a steelheading experience.

The Oyster River and Black Creek, each about fifteen minutes north of Courtenay, are the final watersheds in this tour. Black Creek once produced phenomenal runs of steelhead but these runs seem to have been lost. The Oyster River is notable in the pages of early books on B.C. steelhead. It has runs from December through April but is currently in a very low population phase.

Vancouver Island's multitude of creeks, either tributaries or flowing directly into the sea, provide almost certain success for the young and novice steelheader. These seemingly insignificant creeks, often scoffed at by the uninitiated or the neophyte, are often favored by the Fishhawks for their sure action.

Many of these creeks are complete systems in themselves, having their own headwater watershed and emptying directly into the ocean. Some are well known for their steelhead populations. The better known being: the Ash River, which enters the Stamp just above Money's Pool; China Creek, south of Port Alberni; French

Creek, immediately north of Parksville; Waukwaas Creek, a complete watershed near the Marble River; and Cous Creek, in the Alberni Inlet. Many others are well known by local steelheaders but are not too well known by visiting anglers. Some of these, like Draw Creek, Kaipit Creek, and Haslam Creek, have small populations of wild steelhead. Other productive small creeks are tributaries to major rivers and are often the nurseries for these river highways.

Access along all these creeks or tributaries is usually very difficult because of the heavy coastal undergrowth along the creek banks. However, they display in miniature all conditions the angler will find on the larger streams and rivers and are ideal learning laboratories. The angler fishing these small creeks must be prepared for some hazards which he will not find on a larger stream. Also, the normal tackle used on large streams can become very awkward when fished on these small creeks. But, the small size of the pools is a boon to attaining steelhead know how. The pools do give the angler the opportunity to learn the fundamental rules of reading the water. The holts in each pool are very specific, easy to locate with only a few casts and drifts and easy to memorize. Holding water will be limited and every stretch of olive green water, no matter how small, must be fished until the angler is certain he knows the lies.

When steelhead are hooked they are a real challenge on these small creeks. The small compact pools are often treated with destain by large and active steelhead. After the first run they will try to leave the pool and run downstream around a riverbend usually overgrown with heavy salmonberry brush. It is almost inevitable that these leaping trophies will cause the line to tangle in overgrown brush near the shore if they are not fought with extreme care. A short, stiff rod with a minimum of twenty-pound test line is a must if you are to hold these fish.

I have often found that the steelhead kelt is truly a challenge on these small creeks. They seem to be voracious and gluttonous feeders on their seaward journey and often literally slash at bait, lures, and flies. Labelled "racehorses" because of this activity, they will bolt from their holt and race downstream or up in a terrifying manner. When finally controlled, they will sulk and then, in a last effort, tear once more through the short run, pulling the overwrought angler into the stream as he tries to ease the strain on his tackle.

Vancouver Island's small creeks and streams provide a steel-heading experience unmatched by the larger rivers. They are an angler's master classroom which hasten the learning skills in a manner only experience can appreciate.

In the following short sections about specific steelhead streams, presented alphabetically, I hope to provide one small source of information for both the managers and the novice steelheader. I have chosen twelve representative streams: streams that are managed for wild steelhead and streams dominated by hatchery (urban) steelhead; streams easily accessible and streams which present all that is the wilderness experience in the truest sense for the steelheader; streams that have very few steelhead and streams which are in the top ten producers in the province. Each is unique, yet each provided steel-heading experiences which have become indelible memories for this steelheader. I sincerely hope that they will help to open the gate to a vast river of tradition, knowledge, and site-specific data.

Browns River

The Browns River is a unique river system, home to a rare race of winter steelhead who have evolved to accommodate late season high water run-off. Recently, the Browns River has received world-wide fame as the location of the now famous fossilized *Elasmosaur* which was discovered on the shale banks near where the Browns River enters the Puntledge River.

Steelhead the Browns when the dogwoods bloom! This was the advice I heeded over a quarter of a century ago when I first explored this fascinating tributary of the Puntledge River. My first trip was preceded by almost a century by Dr. Robert Brown, for whom the river is named. In 1862, Dr. Brown headed up an expedition sent to the Comox Valley by the B.C. colonial government for scientific and exploratory purposes. Dr. Brown appears to have not found any major fossils, nor did he record that he fished while exploring the river although he did fish for sturgeon in the Puntledge. However, he did find a wide exposed coal seam which confirmed the existence of large coal deposits in the area and eventually lead to the development of the Comox Valley.

During the winter months, wet coastal southeast storms have little effect on the very low stream flows of the Browns River for its feeding high elevation tributaries are normally encased in fresh snow. These winter low flows, coupled with December, January, and February cold, are likely the limiting factor for salmonid populations in the river. Ground ice is common at this time of the year and steelhead fry hidden in the river bottom gravel often succumb to the slow seeping freezing cold. It is only in late spring, when the Forbidden Plateau snowpack begins to melt, that the river's flow increases. At this time, usually late in April and during the wildflower blooms of May when clusters of trilliums, heavily scented fawn lilies and tiny yellow violets bloom, the adult steelhead enter the Browns River to complete their life odyssey.

This very late run of true winter steelhead is unique to Vancouver Island and has evolved as the result of the particular characteristics of the Browns River watershed. The river and tributaries all flow from mountain snow melt water coming from the Forbidden Plateau. These feeding rivulets originate above 1,000 meter elevation, the result of spring warmth, and cascade rapidly down cliff and canyon to eventually join to form the Browns River.

Specific fishing pools and holding water are limited in the lower four kilometers of river floodplain. This appears due to the sandstone bottom of the river bed which is almost devoid of gravel. Yet, in ways only nature understands and accommodates, a healthy population of gunmetal-colored spring steelhead do survive.

For the steelheader wishing to fish the Browns, every stretch of deeper water, regardless of depth, should be treated as a holding run. It has been my experience that when conditions are ideal, when the stream appears high and slightly colored, virtually every sizable stream rock is a holt for these unique steelhead.

For those wishing to explore the Browns River, access is available from the Forbidden Plateau Road or from the angler's trail, created by the Comox Valley Chapter of the Steelhead Society of B.C., alongside the Puntledge River. Private land does exist along the riverbank and must be respected by all. One spectacular section of river to visit is the Medicine Bowl, a waterfall upstream from the Duncan Bay mainline

Gunter Lill holds a twelve-pound Tsitika-run Campbell River summer steelhead just prior to release. Today the primary angling ethic for steelheaders is catch and release.

Gunter plays a Tsitika-stock summer steelhead on the Campbell River.

The helicopter takes a run along the upper Salmon River.

The author, in the foreground, and partner both fight summer steelhead hooked fly-fishing on the Campbell River.

Summer steelhead hooked with bright fly patterns. Note the downturned eye, a sure sign these fish are alive and well.

The author fly casting on the Gold River.

Barry Thornton Jr. releases a gunmetal winter steelhead in the large boulder-strewn Gold River.

Spawning 'dress' of the December summer steelhead.

Barry Thornton Jr. fishes a magic summer steelhead pool on the White River.

Jim Grinder plays a winter steelhead in the tannin water of the Nahwitti.

The elk meadows of the upper White Valley, south of Stewart Lake. This is a major salmonid nursery in the watershed. Note the insensitive logging done right to the edge of the meadow in the foreground of the picture.

A beached fresh-run Eve River doe steelhead of about twelve pounds. Note the chrome silver on the exposed body and the net or seal scar along the lower side. This fish was quickly released after the photo was taken.

Lew Carswell holds a giant thirty-pound Salmon River winter steelhead prior to its release.

The author swims the upper White River with Fish & Wildlife staff on a summer steelhead count.

The author selects a bright fly for winter steelhead fly-fishing.

The Campbell Pink—a most effective wet fly for both summer and winter steelhead.

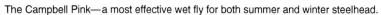

This male steelhead from the Puntledge River shows the red cheek colors and the hooked kype typical of spawning rainbow trout.

Lew and his daughter Leian share a fishing moment while Leian plays a large Salmon River steelhead.

A rare double on summer steelhead.

Previous Page: Ross Ruthven plays a winter steelhead on the Gold River.

Fisheries staff load helicopter drop buckets with steelhead fry for

This wild steelhead, notable for its adipose fin, is carefully slid into a river containment tube prio to being transported to a tank truck.

transplanting to inaccessible Salmon River watershed waters.

Two Oyster River 'wild' steelhead rest in a tank truck while en route to the hatchery.

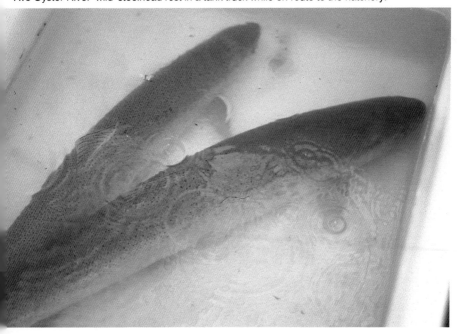

Steelhead management has changed considerably during the past two decades and now includes special river programs and regulations.

logging road. This is a very popular, but extremely dangerous, sight-seeing section with fast water and sheer slippery cliffs. But, for the steelhead angler, it is the lower section of the river immediately above the powerline which is the most productive and popular.

Shirtsleeve weather, clusters of trilliums and flowering dog-woods are all synonymous with spring steelheading on the Browns River.

Unfortunately, at this writing, the Puntledge River and hence the Browns have been placed on a total angling closure to protect the now rare races of steelhead which inhabit this watershed. Much work is being done to correct this decline but, for the foreseeable future, steelheaders can only sit on the riverbank when the dogwoods bloom and dream of what was and what might be.

Campbell River

Visualize this journey taken by summer steelhead on the Campbell River; a female steelhead is caught in the Tsitika River on the northeast coast of Vancouver Island during August by sports angling. She is then transported south by a fisheries tank truck, 225 miles to the provincial hatchery at Duncan. Here she is held until she is ready to spawn in February. Then she is stripped of her eggs and, at the same time, a male steelhead, also sports caught from the Tsitika River, is milked of his sperm and the eggs are fertilized.

These fertilized eggs are then placed in incubation trays, hatched in May and then held until they have reached the fry stage sometime in July. The fry are then transported by fisheries tank truck back to the North Island, 300 miles this time, to be reared in holding pens in O'Connor Lake. Here they stay for the next two years until they are nearing the smoltification stage in May.

At this time, now weighing sixty to seventy grams, they are again placed in a fresh water fisheries tank truck and are trucked south, 175 miles to the Campbell River. Here they are released in the waters somewhere below the B.C. Hydro power dam so that they will home to the waters of the Campbell River on their return spawning journey.

Once in the Campbell River the steelhead smolts begin a slow drift downriver until they have entered the sea in the saltwater of Discovery Passage. Through the process of smoltification they have adapted to the saline waters of the Pacific Ocean and they begin a slow journey north out into the open Pacific through Johnstone Strait.

Two, three, four, and even five years later, following an epic odyssey in the North Pacific, they again travel south through Johnstone Strait and enter the estuary of the Campbell River sometime during June through November.

A success story? Yes! You only have to see and watch the many fly-fishing steelheaders in the upper waters of the Campbell River every summer and autumn to know that these Tsitika River summer steelhead are providing a fly-fishing utopia.

But, why this incredible summer steelhead fishery; why the Campbell River?

In correspondence and discussions with George Reid, Vancouver Island Head, Fisheries, Ministry of Environment, Lands & Parks, he stated that the following steps were taken by MOE:

In 1978, we (MOE) reviewed summer steelhead enhancement opportunities throughout the entire east coast of Vancouver Island. Parameters looked at included mean summer flow, maximum water temperature, steelhead catch history, public access, fishability, water development (logging, etc.), and brood stock availability.

Under the rating system developed in that study, Campbell River was selected as the best opportunity for fishery development.

In the fall of 1978, we conducted a pilot program to capture, transport, and hold Tsitika River summer run adults.
These fish were successfully held and spawned.

After establishing the program's acceptability and feasibility the next step was implementation.

In October and November of 1980, Tsitika adults were again captured and held.

The fry resulting from this exercise were reared to smolt stage in net pens at O'Connor Lake (northern Vancouver Island) and released into the Campbell River.

The rest is history.

When the decision was made by MOE to enhance summer steelheading opportunity on the east coast of Vancouver Island, a second decision was made to provide limited entry fly-fishing only in the upper waters of the Campbell River, the famous "Upper" and "Lower" Island pools. These were the waters most often frequented by Roderick Haig-Brown, the waters most often mentioned in his famous angling literature.

This was a conscious decision and one which at that time took considerable courage by fisheries managers. No other steelhead river system in British Columbia had a designated fly-fishing tackle restriction at that time.

George Reid provides the following explanation:

The arguments against establishing a fly-fishing only section were:
1. It is discriminatory.
2. Hatchery fish were placed in the river to satisfy a kill fishery.

We sided with what I believed were the enlightened fishermen who argued that the establishment of a fly-fishing 'no-kill' fishery stressed quality.

They also argued that those values were consistent with the writings and principles of Roderick Haig-Brown.

Again, the rest is history!

The Campbell River is a controlled flow river first dammed and developed by B.C. Hydro in 1947. It is a large river for Vancouver Island, with high water flows up to 4,400 cubic feet per second. Most Vancouver Island streams have high flows measuring less than 1,000 cubic feet per second.

Cooperation between the Ministry of Environment, Lands & Parks and B.C. Hydro has been established to provide high quality summer steelhead fly-fishing. MOE has requested that summer flows be kept low to slow the upstream migration of the Tsitika stock summer steelhead in order that they spread out throughout the Campbell and not jam up at the John Hart Dam outflow. B.C. Hydro is to be commended for their cooperation in this fishery where they have attempted to keep flows as low as 1,200 cubic feet per second during summer months.

In an interview with B.C. Hydro, they did tell me that water conditions are dictated by the mountain snow pack and rains in January and February. These water conditions determine the spillage in the summer from various holding reservoirs and hence, the released summer daily flows.

Anglers should be warned that sirens placed along the river sound when water flows are to be increased! It has been my experience in the past that this will occur daily during the summer. Be warned; the B.C. Hydro manager told me of one angler who was treed for eight hours one day on the lower island when he did not heed the alarm and continued to fish in the river.

Daily flow changes are beneficial for the fly angler, for the change of flows will move the steelhead. They often shift from deeper runs and pools to the more fishable shallows where the fly-fisherman has a much more effective chance to cover them with his wet and dry fly offerings.

I first fished for steelhead on the Campbell River during the mid-1960s. At that time I was also fortunate to meet Roderick Haig-Brown. As the years passed our paths crossed on numerous occasions: at B.C. Wildlife Federation Conventions where I was the Director chairing the Steelhead Committee; at numerous Steelhead Society of B.C. meetings, workshops and "fish tanks" while I was a Director and President. During the time I served as President of the S.S.B.C., Rod was a member of an informal advisory committee which met in our homes and which did much to formulate S.S.B.C. policies.

I have continued to fish the Campbell River each year since those earlier years. I have been fortunate in that I have been able to experience the incredible Tsitika stock/Campbell River summer steelhead fly-fishery since the first year of the return of these fish. The large concentrations of returning steelhead have given me the opportunity to experiment with all forms of fly lines including shooting heads, sink tips, and floating lines. All, I have found, have their own place for summer steelhead fishing. I have also had the opportunity to experiment with many fly patterns, both wet and dry, and have found these large magnificent Tsitika steelhead eager to take my offerings in those favored upper and lower island pools.

I have watched many anglers fly-fishing these waters and, with each fish hooked and released, I often think of Rod. I know that he would approve of the "catch-and-release" trend.

In my personal correspondence with Rod two decades ago, he made the following comment on catch-and-release.

> Steelhead fishermen would do well to consider the possibilities of a catch-and-release program. This could be by regulation on streams where there is shown to be below-capacity spawning escapement. It could be encouraged everywhere as a means of improving sport throughout the season, as the fishing intensity on most accessible streams is now great enough to prevent any significant build up of fish in the pools. Steelhead are not inclined to become hook-shy and one fish can be caught several times.

I know he would be proud to have his river managed in this manner, to preserve the dignity of fly-fishing and for the preservation of our magnificent steelhead trout!

Eve River

The low, clear stream water demanded a change of terminal tackle and I reluctantly tied on a small #8 hook with eight-pound test leader. It is always a gamble to use light leader when fishing for winter steelhead for you never know what size of fish will strike or with what circumstances you will be faced.

The run I was drifting with my float was ideal as a steelhead holt. It contained large boulders, a straight slick beside the main current, and a section of deep green-colored water. It had all the markings of a steelhead lie and, when the float disappeared on the first drift through, I knew it held a fish.

Carefully, but with the intense excitement of a hunter when he has at long last sighted his prey, I rebaited the hook, tested the leader, then cast again. The torpedo-shaped float with its bright red top angled downstream in the shallower water as it drifted to the run, momentarily hung perpendicular as it floated through the deep holt, then slowly but irresistibly sank underwater. The main line was taunt to the float from the rod tip as I firmly lifted the rod tip upward. A brief eternal moment occurred as the rod held bowed to the quarry. Then, a sudden shudder vibrated through the rod as the fish tested the force pulling at it. Realizing the danger, it leapt—a magnificent steelhead—its mauve metallic hue glistening as it threw spray in a web around the river. Then, as if it had sighted the hunter during its wondrous leap, it streaked downstream making a siren of the reel.

A submerging log angling downstream from the far bank was the shelter it sought in the clear water. I snubbed the reel in an attempt to turn the incredible strength but to no avail. It knew that under the log lay its only safety and even though it began to tire in its arrow dash, the light leader and increasing arc of the rod foretold that it would be safe. Under the log the fallen branches caught on my weights and the rod snapped straight.

I was fishing the Eve River on a long overdue trip. It had been some time since I had last played a prime sixteen-pound doe on one of the lower pools. It was the haunting memory of that spectacular wild fish, which snapped at my bait offering numerous times before she was finally hooked, ran through the tailout and then dashed along a boulder strewn sandbar fighting to reach the safety of the ocean, that drew me back to this sparkling river. My partner and I were on an exploratory trip searching for access points on this fabled north Island stream renowned for its big fish and late winter runs. On this memorable trip we did hook a number of premigrant steelhead smolts which appeared to have just emerged from hibernation in the river gravel. They were all dark, like spawning rainbow trout found in lakes. We were amazed at their length and released one which measured eleven inches.

The Eve River is relatively short, like most Island streams, between ten and fifteen miles in length and comparable in width to the Oyster, the Quinsam and the Qualicums. In the lower two miles, however, it widens on a narrow flood plain and is strengthened by the addition of the Adam River.

The Adam is fishable for only a short distance upstream from its confluence with the Eve, then a canyon and falls block access for both fish and man. This fishable section of the Adam should not be ignored by the angler as good runs of steelhead move into the few pools in this lower part of the river.

The Eve River, on the other hand, has no natural barriers and provides good fishing along its entire length. It has runs of both summer and winter steelhead although summer-run fish are few in comparison.

A highly exciting Pink salmon fly-fishery in the estuary of the Eve River once drew fly anglers from throughout North America. I recall spending an afternoon with an angler from Connecticut who told me that this was a choice location for members of his fly-fishing club. Regulations, due to excessive commercial salmon fishing in Johnstone Strait, do limit sport fishing opportunity in August when the Pinks are schooling at the river mouth.

Like the west coast streams of Vancouver Island, the Eve is a large boulder stream which does make wading difficult. Beginning in April, like most Island streams, it also has a heavy algae growth which makes it almost mandatory for the angler to wear felt soles or cleats if he is to do any serious wading on the slippery rocks.

In recent years the Vancouver Island Highway linking the north Island with the south has been completed. The highway follows the upper valley of the Eve River and does provide a number of access locations to the upper river as well as logging mainline road access to the lower river.

My many trips to the Adam and Eve rivers, since the first road access became available in the mid-1970s, have given me a fond appreciation of this magnificent watershed. Roosevelt elk, blacktail deer, river otters and killer whales have all provided special experiences, along with the river's large steelhead fished in crystal clear waters. The Eve River is a sleeper, a river of destiny which, as it recovers from massive logging clearcuts, will be a river which will provide steelheading experiences sought after by anglers from around North America.

Gold River

On Vancouver Island when steelheaders talk of favored streams and big wild steelhead, the discussion inevitably centers on the Gold River. It was here, in March of 1974, that Bruce Gerhart beached a thirty-pound trophy male steelhead, one of the largest winter steelhead ever recorded from a Vancouver Island stream. A scale sample from this fish showed a seven-year life span, a 2.5 fish; that is, a fish who had spent two years in fresh water and five years in salt water. It was also a first spawner.

The Gold River is an outstanding all-year steelheading stream with runs of winter and summer steelhead entering the river every month. Peak runs occur at specific times: in December, March, April, May, and September. But these vary and are dependent upon water conditions in the stream.

The watershed of the Gold River is extensive for an Island stream. Headwater tributaries start in the heart of the Sutton Range and the northern peaks of the Vancouver Island Mountain Range. Rising in the spine of the Island at Gold Lake, the river is surrounded by Vancouver Island's second highest mountains: Victoria Peak (7,095 ft.), Horseshoe Mountain (5,700 ft.), and Waring Peak (5,252 ft.).

Four major river systems act as tributaries to the Gold River creating the sparkling and unique color so obvious throughout its lower courses. The first to meet the Gold is the Muchalat River flowing out of Muchalat Lake. This is a river system that historically produced large numbers of chinook and sockeye salmon, as well as steelhead. The second system, the Upana meets the Gold about five miles downstream. Its watershed takes in all northern waters from Big Baldy Mountain (5,285 ft.) visible across the town site. The third system, the Heber River, originating on the western mountain slopes of Strathcona Park, was made famous by Roderick Haig-Brown for its summer steelhead fishery. It was here that he perfected his dry fly, the Western Bee. Unfortunately, B.C. Hydro's diversion of Heber water for its Campbell Lakes/Elk Fall Hydro-Hydra complex virtually dries this classic stream during low summer flows. This abuse, coupled with the grotesque clearcut streambank logging in the watershed and along the stream's main watercourse, has almost destroyed the runs of summer fish and left only a residual run to restock the system. Finally, downstream below the lower canyon and about two miles from the estuary, the Ucona River enters the Gold at one of the most productive steelhead runs.

It is interesting to note, historically, that it was on the Heber River in the early seventies that catch-and-release was first tried as a management tool for steelhead. At that time, the fledgling Steelhead Society of B.C. convinced the Fisheries managers that rather than close the river and the opportunity to fish, they adopt an experimental catch-and-release program for the summer-run steelhead on the Heber River. Arguments were provided which showed that steelhead did recover in twenty-four to forty-eight hours after being hooked and, that with the use of barbless hooks, the survival rate would be more than 90 percent. Thanks to the support of V.I. Director Charley Lyons and V.I. Fisheries biologist George Reid, the experiment was tried and worked.

One of my cherished stretches of water is the easily accessible Ucona Run. It is a long stretch of fly-fishing water which takes many pleasurable hours to cover. Starting at the mouth of the Ucona River, about 500 yards upstream from the car park, a wide crescent pool flows downstream, shallows in mid river where a side channel flows up against sweeping evergreen boughs and then deepens into a trough which rejoins the main river at a stand of rock. Steelhead seem to favor this side channel when the river is colored.

I have found that this magic stretch of water holds steelhead at any time of the day. I like to think that this is tidal water even though it is more than a mile from the Pacific Ocean and not subject to water changes in level. It is so like those special upstream holding pools in the estuarian section of every river where steelhead will come to rest prior to deciding whether they will move further upstream or drop back into the sea. For that reason I have found I can fish this stretch any time of the day and know that there will be fresh fish in the water.

Many fly runs are available on the Gold for the "hunting" steelheading fly-fisherman. The natural river bottom, large boulders of basketball size and bigger, provide many steelhead holding runs and slots. Water levels are constantly changing as is water clarity.

These are the major factors which determine where steelhead will rest as they move throughout this watershed. To become familiar with the system, it is important that the fly-fisher hike the river in all conditions. This is an angling adventure in itself for it is known there are always steelhead holding in the Gold River every day of the year.

A second special fly-fishing area that I treasure lies on the long stretch below the Muchalat pools, that very fishy area now commonly known as "Branch 14." Angling tradition provides names for river pools following years of angling. The Gold, being such a new system, still finds itself going through this naming transitional period. What was once known as the "A-Frame" pools now bears the name "Branch 14" or "Muchalat" pools.

The long section of river downstream from where the Gold River and the larger Muchalat River merge, is the location of my second choice area and it is water that can take a full day to fly-fish and still, there will be sections not covered. Depending upon water levels and color, and these change on a regular basis, steelhead will hold in every trough and behind every large boulder in this lengthy and challenging water! I prefer to start at the head of the these runs when I fly-fish, working my way downstream, casting to each slot, trough, boulder, and deeper green water that I find. This is a lengthy process but, for me, has proven to be highly successful.

Downriver, below the town site, pool names often change each year, as I talk to new anglers on the river. Regardless of names, however, the riverbank of the Gold River appears not to change to any great degree below the town site. As a result, the traditional steelhead holding waters also remain the same in these lower waters.

The Gold River is recognized as one of British Columbia's aquatic gems! It is situated on the west coast of Vancouver Island and lies at the head of Muchalat Inlet, near Nootka Island, the location of first contact in the 1700s by the Spaniards and then English with First Nation races. It is an interesting thought that these early Europeans may also have fished this aquatic treasure for they were so close and at that time, the late 1700s, angling traditions had been formed in their countries.

One of the outstanding features of the Gold River is that it provides access to fish along its total length. A major paved road, leading to the Pulp Mill at the estuary, follows the riverbank and river gorge. Sometimes it is right beside the river, while at others, it is above the bank but close enough for an easy walk except in the main canyon. The canyon must be seen to be appreciated and only in my early steelheading years did I challenge its cardiac courses.

The Gold River is Vancouver Island's premier wild steelhead river. With the introduction of steelhead hatchery programs on Vancouver Island in the early 1970s, the Fisheries Branch made a conscious decision to keep the Gold River free of hatchery fish. This decision was supported by organized anglers including the Steelhead Society of B.C. and the B.C. Wildlife Federation. The fact that this has been the right decision is amply shown by the Vancouver Island angler catch graph.

I would add my own personal support for this management decision by the Fisheries Branch. I strongly believe that any decision to add hatchery stock to the Gold River would mark the end of that unique quality of wild fish which the Gold River offers to the adventurous steelhead angler.

The Gold River, like its southern more popular sister the Stamp River, is a river with good runs of both summer and winter steelhead. But, unlike the Stamp River which has received a heavy hatchery program, almost all steelhead on the Gold are wild steelhead. The Gold River is unique on Vancouver Island for it is a river with runs of steelhead which prefer to hold in the lower section of the river. Parts of that lower canyon are inaccessible but other sections will astound you for the number of fish that they repeatedly hold every month of the year!

The Gold River is the one steelhead stream which fully epitomizes steelhead angling on Vancouver Island. The Gold has suffered all the gross land use problems common to Vancouver Island streams and yet, it still supports an extensive fishery. The Gold must remain the epitome of the Pacific Northwest steelheading experience! It must receive stronger land use and water quality protection to preserve it as a "wild" river.

Little Qualicum River

Despite the quantity and quality of steelhead streams available to the Vancouver Island steelheader it is difficult to find time to investigate more than a few favorite ones each season. Variety and opportunity are certainly the prerogative of the Island steelheader.

I plan at least one major fishing trip annually to the Little Qualicum, to reminisce, for it was on this exciting stream that I beached my first steelhead in 1960. My experience was typical of all uninitiated coastal stream fishermen who first attempt to fish Island rivers with light trout tackle. I was spin casting at the estuary of the river, looking for cutthroat trout which I had heard were prevalent there during April. I was using six-pound test monofilament line with a small silver spinner when a fresh-run steelhead took the lure and streaked out of the pool towards the saltchuck. It was a small fish, about five pounds, and in the shallow low tide delta he raced from pool to pool anxious to reach the safety of the ocean. My light tackle had little affect on the fish and I am certain today that I beached him only because he tired from having to race such a distance to reach the ocean at low tide. Since that first trip I have spent hundreds of hours on the Little Qualicum and remember them as some of my most exciting and enjoyable steelheading experiences.

My diary reminds me of one typical March day with two fellow steelheaders on this most pleasant steelhead stream.

We parked our truck at the Power Line, one access point to the river, and fished through the meadows up to the Glory Hole. This was an exploratory trip and we had committed ourselves to fish the unfamiliar waters along this stretch of the river. The water was in prime condition and the clear winter day and open meadows created the atmosphere for what was to be an exciting and memorable day.

Starting at the Power Line Pool we began to pool hop; that is, we would each fish a separate pool and then move upstream searching every known holt for a fish. Throughout the day we found the fish scattered in pockets. At the run immediately below Dolly Varden creek one partner rolled a bright fish but was unable to hook it again when it sulked somewhere in the run. Above the creek is a section of water which seems to be a major holding area for steelhead and here we beached two good fish. The first, a bright doe of eight pounds, took at my feet as I was retrieving my lure after a drift in mid stream. Angling conditions on the Little Qualicum River are unique. The river is fed from Cameron Lake with waters that are often uniquely creamy. This water condition looks similar to glacial run-off but is caused by a highly colloidal clay in the headwaters of Cameron Creek. This dissolved clay turns the water a blue-gray cream color similar to the color of milk in coffee. When the river is in this condition, steelhead will frequently hold in the very shallow sections of the water, often literally at your feet.

Our second fish was a big buck steelhead, close to eighteen pounds, which took on a shallow drift through a slick immediately below some overhanging alder branches. It was a heavy fish which twice ran out downstream from holding pools. It fought doggedly and when it was finally beached my partner disengaged the hook with a pair of needlenose pliers and eased the trophy back in the river.

We crossed the river then and entered the unknown waters between the open meadow and the Glory Hole. In many places we found that we had to break a trail through thickets of eight-foot-high salmonberry stalks and dangerous devil's club stems. Unlike the developed meadow and the river trails in the canyon areas, there was no trail in this section other than occasional game trails which led near the river and along the bluffs of the river basin. Upstream, we fought our way through the heavy thickets along the river's edge and finally reached a log jam. On the beach below the dam we collected two Peterson's disk salmon tags left there from salmon tagged in the ocean by the Federal Department of Fisheries. Upstream, pools and log jams made fishing almost impossible. We hooked one fish but quickly lost it as it dashed under a jam of logs and branches. A wide side channel offering excellent potential for rearing salmon and steelhead fry was a second barrier. We had to take a half mile detour before we could again reach the river. Long runs prevailed in this area with obvious signs of steelhead redds scattered in the gravel. One long excellent flycasting run yielded two more steelhead, all bright and very active. Pool hopping upstream, we soon entered a section with many bends and many holding pools. At the first pool, we cast towards an ancient log jutting out downstream from the bank. Here a bright fish suddenly struck the lure and then water-walked up and down the pool. On the second run, still dolphining on the pool surface, it broke the line, much to the chagrin of my partner who had palmed his Silex too firmly. We rolled two more fish heading upstream and then reached the section of the river known as the Glory Hole. An old logging road led down to this pool and it was along this and the angler's trail that we headed back to the road and our truck.

The Little Qualicum River has received a strong infusion of hatchery steelhead during the past decade and these fish have provided outstanding angling on this river. A major hatchery complex, situated a few miles down Melrose Road with access off the Island Highway between Parksville and Port Alberni, has done much to improve all salmonids in the Little Qualicum River.

There are four major points of access to the Little Qualicum River for the angler. To fish the estuary and mouth of the stream access can be gained from the Island Highway bridge. Fishing water is limited below the bridge.

Since the introduction of hatchery steelhead to the river, the most productive section of water is between the Island Highway bridge and the railroad bridge. Access to this area is from the pumphouse area. Angling trails follow both sides of the river and it seems that any deep pocket of water holds steelhead.

Access to beautiful canyon pools and the famous Whiskey Creek pool, located immediately above the railroad bridge, can be obtained by turning off at the store about a quarter of a mile north of the Island Highway bridge. Drive to the railway tracks, follow them and park, then walk south along the tracks to the river. A cardiac hill to the river is easy on the way down but most difficult up! In the canyon, a well-traveled fisherman's trail follows the river past the Whiskey Creek pool to an open valley which is the lower section of the meadows.

The Island Highway leading to Port Alberni gives access to the upper meadows at the Power Line Pool and the Dolly Varden Run. Follow the signs marking the Little Qualicum hatchery, located one mile south of the Whiskey Creek store. Turn north on Melrose Road and follow this improved road until you reach the hatchery site. Access up and down the river is possible from this location.

The stream banks throughout the meadow are all fenced and fishermen should use the stiles which were built by the Qualicum Fish & Game Club to cross these fences. Stiles were placed at every pool along the meadow section of the river. As well as saving fences, these stiles are a simple indicator of the major pools and runs in this area of the river.

Melrose Road also gives access to the Glory Hole and its once well-tramped angler trails. A little over two miles from the highway, turn left on a side road. Follow this as far as possible, then walk the half hour to the Glory Hole. Excellent steelhead pools and runs are located both upstream and downstream from this point.

In the upper reaches of the Little Qualicum, deep pools and log jams provide excellent rearing areas for resident trout. Summer fly-fishing and spin-fishing are an added bonus on this beautiful stream. As an additional bonus, brown trout also reside in the Little Qualicum, coming from stock planted in Cameron Lake in the 1920s. This is an extremely wary trout but catches of browns weighing from one to four pounds have been noted on this stream.

Nahwitti River

The first time I fished for steelhead on the Nahwitti I had the strange experience of pool hopping with a helicopter. My partners and I had hiked through the second canyon below the lake and had reached a rare open bank area on the stream. We were exhausted from slip-sliding along rock-faced walls but were at last at a section of the river where we were hooking steelhead. The stream area where we found ourselves fishing merged with tributary streams and this was where the fish were holding. But, our success was to be short lived!

My partner had just hooked a good steelhead and we were standing watching the aerial display of this hard-fighting fish when we heard the "thuck-thuck-thuck" of helicopter blades. Within moments, a guided party of anglers had landed on the beach by the next pool about 200 meters below us.

When we finished fishing the pool, we detoured through the virgin mature timber beyond their prime crescent pool, where we did observe one angler playing a fish, and downstream to fish what appeared to be a holding run. However, we soon heard the helicopter again and watched it fly over us and proceed downstream to land at another beach pool another 200 meters downstream.

We had a long hike back to our vehicle and decided to return to the camper rather than try to compete with this mode of angling.

Since that first trip, I have been back to the Nahwitti many times. The memory of pristine wilderness, riverbank elk trails, tannin brown water and bright wild steelhead have been the lure. The logging company, Richmond Plywood, which first opened the river waters below that first impassable canyon has now pushed a road past the second canyon and beyond. Each year the road, now following both sides of the river, gets closer and closer to the estuary and has provided public access to a magnificent river for steelheaders. A knowledgeable steelheader I met on the river did tell me that it is now but a two day river fishing trip to reach the estuary.

The Nahwitti River is the most northern river on Vancouver Island, flowing directly north east into Hecate Strait. It is situated approximately half-way between Cape Scott Provincial Park and the community of Port Hardy. Access to the river is along a gravel highway. It is a small-to medium-sized river with Nahwitti Lake as its prime source of water. Downstream from the lake a number of tributary streams, Camp Creek, Fennel Creek, Godkin Creek, and others swell the main river and create major steelheading pools for the angler.

Hiking the river is a major challenge to any angler. The stream has cut a narrow gorge through the valley bottom. Heavy overhanging tree roots and shrubs make it virtually impossible to climb up and out of the river course. During periods of low water, an angler can follow the river beach walking on rocks that vary from the size of a basketball to a small table top, depending on the stream gradient. Rocks are layered, a new observation to me during my most recent trip; that is, as one looked mid way downriver it was obvious that the force of the water during high flows had embedded one stone upon another, much like ruffled scales. While river wading is difficult most of the time, the rock layering does permit walking downstream, much like stepping down stairs, but the return upstream is upstairs all the way.

Elk trails do follow the riverbank but these tend to be short in nature and disappear when small beachside openings occur. Following these trails in chest waders is a major feat, particularly with the many fallen logs, some immense forest giants, which must be climbed or detoured.

Pools are scattered and do require lengthy hikes by the steelheader. The river water is a heavy tannin color and makes the river bottom very difficult to see or gage. This, however, is an advantage for the fish! During periods of low flows, I have hooked steelhead in the fast water shallows in areas where I often felt it was impossible for a fish to hold. Obvious holding pools and runs are usually well defined and my experience has shown that they regularly hold many fish.

While the above may appear masochistic to the average fisherman, to the steelheader the Nahwitti is a river of dreams! A good population of wild steelhead travel throughout the river from December through April. These are good fish averaging more than four kilograms and are explosive when hooked. I am certain a summer run also enters the river judging from the deep rainbow red colored spawners that I have often hooked, beached, and released.

Like all rivers with which steelheaders are afflicted, the following memory is one of the many lures which draws me annually to take one or more steelheading trips to the Nahwitti.

The bank was about three meters above the river run with just enough room between towering fallen log roots for a back swing so that I could cast with my single action Silex outfit. On the first drift the float hung straight up and down, a sign that my lure was not reaching the bottom. On the retrieve, I slid the cork float further up the fluorescent green Stren main line to extend the depth of the Gooey-bob lure so that it drifted along the bottom rocks.

On the second drift, by watching the angle and drift of the float, I was able to determine the best possible steelhead lie, the deepest slot in the run where the water flowed with equal speed, the location for a holding steelhead. Casting for a third time, as I now had the right depth because, on the last drift, the float had angled downstream, I placed the terminal tackle at the head of the run and reeled to eliminate all slack line in order to hold the mainline directly to the float.

Two thirds of the way down the run the float suddenly submerged, disappearing in the tea-colored water. My strike was instinctive but I was startled by the explosion of the large doe as she burst out of the water. Before I could fully react she shot down to the tailout, leaped once, twice, and then a third time in the fast water shallows. Each time, instinctively, I bowed to the fish trying at the same time to ease the line pressure as I palmed the single action reel. Feeling this tightening pressure, the fish shot upstream through the depths of the run and out into the fast water shallows above.

It was not until this moment that I felt I had some control over my tackle. I reeled madly to pick up the slack line, thankful that the fish was still moving upstream, keeping line pressure on the barbless hook. In moments, I was at the fish and she turned when she felt the added pressure from my downstream pull. This time, racing downstream, she circled, leapt once in the main run and then shot out of the run heading downstream to the next pool.

This was the last thing I wanted her to do! Downstream, on my side of the river, was an impassable outgrowth of riverbank alders and firs. I tried every trick I knew to bring her back up to the run. I fed slack line to produce a loop of line which would drag at the hook from downstream but this only moved her over to the other side of the river where she held in a slot under overhanging salmonberry brush. I reeled tight and, after creating a pressure bend in the rod, began a slow walk upstream trying to "walk" her back to the run without the line jerking, caused by reel retrieving. She came about ten meters but, then, fought against the steady pressure and darted downstream to once again lie below the overhanging salmonberry.

I was now at the point of cutting my mainline and attaching a second float to the cut end, a trick I have used on occasion with a high success rate. When I do this, I pull out slack line to create a downstream line loop to hold the barbless hook. Then, I attach a large float to the cut end of the mainline and throw this out into the middle of the river so that the drifting line will clear the downstream barrier. Watching and following this float downstream, I move past the barrier and then cast a weight across the line. Reeling this line in,

I then attach it to my mainline and I am now able to play the fish from downstream.

However, with this magnificent steelhead I tried a fourth and final trick, a downstream walk in the middle of the river. While I was not certain what changes had occurred to this particular run since the last time I fished the river, it was obvious that the downstream area where the fish was holding was only a meter or so deep.

Gingerly stepping down the riverbank I eased into the river, testing each step. At every opportunity I reeled in slack line. I was wearing tungsten cleats and, as I felt the ever increasing pressure of the river, the cleats gripped the slippery river rocks firmly. My third leg, my wading staff, gave me ample opportunity to brace myself against the current with each new step. Meanwhile, the steelhead held firm in the salmonberry slot.

When I was waist high in the current, beyond the downstream barrier, I began a slow drift downstream bobbing with the current as I looked for a shallowing of the river at the tailout. It was there and, while the main current was now pushing me inexorably downstream, I moved out into the main river. Literally crab walking downstream, I was soon clear of the riverbank obstruction and now able to walk into the more shallow water downstream of the steelhead.

When once again I had my feet planted firmly in knee high water, I gave my full attention to the steelhead. Throughout my downstream drift, I had kept the line firm to the fish and now began a slow pull to take the doe out from under the salmonberry bush and back into the main current. She responded, breaking water in a number of magnificent jumps, but soon she tired and we began the inevitable dogged fight that soon had her at the beach.

On the surface, in shallow water, she lay on her side, a marvellous trophy wild steelhead weighing close to eight kilograms! I carefully eased the barbless hook from the side of her mouth and, when I felt she had recuperated sufficiently to handle the light current in the backwater, I released her.

The Nahwitti, in size, would be classified as somewhat larger than the average Vancouver Island stream. Fisheries information is limited but as logging continues towards the estuary it is becoming more and more obvious this is one of the Island's classic wild steelheading streams which will require more and more site specific management consideration.

Oyster River

I was fishing a new pool on the Oyster River. It had just formed, a result of winter floods washing the unstable riverbanks in the lower two miles. It appeared as a classic pool with good deep green colored-water throughout and a deeper slot running its full length. A steep bank on the far side bordered with sheltering alders gave the fish overhead protection and a sense of security from all but the unfathomable steelhead angler. On previous trips to the river, I had thoroughly tested the run and catalogued it as a certain fish holt with no snags.

I was float-fishing with my matched Hardy Silex reel and Hardy ten-foot mooching rod, a prime steelhead combination. I had rigged my terminal tackle with the remarkably successful small orange Luhr Jensen Gooey-bob; a rubber latex imitation of salmon eggs.

On the newly formed shallows of the river below, a gigantic fir lay on its side, a victim of heavy fall floods. From a scar on its lower trunk I identified it as the uprooted monarch that had stood at the path pool 500 meters upstream. The immense volume of water necessary to dislodge this giant from the riverbank and then float it downstream was incredible!

Already the resident beavers of the Oyster had begun to trim the branches off at the trunk. During the past three decades I have rarely seen these river guardians at work. Theirs is a nocturnal life. Occasionally, on an early morning approach to a pool, I have stimulated a thunderous crack when I startled one at his work. Each year I count my blessings as an angler for their work on the rivers. Unstable riverbanks on the lower reaches of many streams have caused many a prime evergreen, alder or maple to fall into the river and cover a favorite holding pool. Within weeks, however, the beavers have made fishing possible again by clipping the branches and freeing the tree trunks to float downstream.

"Steelhead fever" raced through my veins as I cast to the head of the slot for another drift through this promising pool. This time, I knew that I was not ready when the float submerged, for I had not reeled fast enough with the single action silex to gather in the slack line as my float drifted downstream. With a flash of silver the steelhead rolled and was off!

I rested the pool for a few minutes, re-sharpened my hook for the umpteenth time, then cast to the head of the slot once again.

This time, I hand-stripped the line to keep it free to the float throughout the drift. When the strike came, I lifted the rod tip hard and fast, felt the sudden halt of a fish on, then let the line stream through my fingers. A bright four-kilogram doe cartwheeled throughout the pool! With line to reel I began the earnest struggle which eventually landed the shimmering metallic mauve beauty on the beach. Carefully, I removed the hook and released her to procreate her kind and possibly to embellish another fisherman's day.

An hour later, after drift-fishing other pools unsuccessfully, I waded across the river to fish what can best be described as the bulldozer pool. The past history of this outstanding steelhead pool reads like a gory detective novel. It is enough to say here that the bulldozer which created the present pool is the prime reason why two miles of the lower river changes with each new spate throughout the year. The bulldozer pool has a funnel effect, with a deep slot at its tailout. Here, at present, is the steelhead holt.

The sun broke through a few high marestails and outlined the rocks in the shallow run. It emphasized where the slot was located. My first drift through the run rolled another bright steelhead, but it was an "on-off" fish. I sat on a beach log and gulped a quick cup of coffee from my thermos to settle the quickening steelhead fever. When I was calmed I walked back to the edge of the river and cast again to the slot. This was an active fish! Before I could even set the hook she was on, spinning and rolling in the fastwater tailout section of the run. When she recovered from the first shock she turned about-face and headed downstream with the reel screaming in my hand. At the first bend, 100 meters downstream, I held hard and forced her into the deep merging side channel that joined the river. Like a flashing trophy rainbow in a clear mountain lake, she dogged—cartwheeled—sulked—rolled and nosed the rocks. But the end was inevitable! Twice she fought in vain for the safety of the river current, but she soon lay on the beach, a perfect match to the one released an hour earlier.

If there is one Vancouver Island river which offers every possible variety of winter steelhead angling experiences, it is the Oyster River. The Oyster is my personal home river, that one watershed system where I will spend more than 50 percent of my winter steelheading time.

I first fished this once bountiful system in the mid-1960s when watershed logging concerns were just beginning to be heard by the public. Sadly, the upper watershed of the Oyster was clearcut on steep riverbank slopes and logging roads were pushed along streambank edges. These two man-caused factors quickly altered the natural flows on this river and have left a legacy of silt-laden gravel bottoms inhospitable to salmonid reproduction. Until this silt is flushed from the system and until the riverbank becomes stable, the Oyster will remain, in the steelheader's jargon, a "yo-yo" system with few fish. Fortunately, in recent years through the Salmonid Enhancement Program, a community project, The Oyster River Enhancement Society has provided major stocks of hatchery-raised salmon. This program has raised public awareness to the plight of the river and will act as a stimulant for future environmental protection.

The Oyster River is approximately thirty miles long and like the arterial branches flowing into a tree trunk, there are an infinite number of large and small tributaries flowing into this major river. The four major arterial tributaries, Adrian Creek, Piggot Creek, Woodhus Creek, and the Little Oyster River were formed during the last glacial period thousands of years ago. At that time, a massive mile-deep sheet of ice blanketed most of Vancouver Island and left only a few areas, like Brooks Peninsula and the crowns of some Vancouver Island mountain peaks, ice free.

Mt. Washington (1,590 m), Mt. Adrian (1,870 m), Mt. Albert Edward (2,093 m) and Alexandra Peak (1,982 m), all mountains with slopes feeding tributaries to the Oyster River, were some of the few ice-free land areas. Like islands in the sea, these mountain tops, surrounded and isolated by glacial ice, were home to a few hardy plants and animals in this period of intense cold. Their unique status resulted in the survival of Vancouver Island's rare chocolate brown

Vancouver Island marmot. This glacial period began to recede about 12,000 years ago.

Postglacial time on Vancouver Island is subdivided into three main periods. The first period began about 10,000 years ago and lasted for about 1,500 years. It was characterized by a cold, moist climate. The second period began about 8,500 years ago and was a warm and dry period with higher temperatures. It lasted until about 3,000 years ago. Our current period is a cold, humid fluctuating climate. It is the common maritime climate, characterized by mild temperatures with prolonged cloudy periods and a small range of temperature. It has wet and mild winters, cool and relatively dry summers and a long frost-free season. Heavy precipitation occurs during the late fall and winter seasons.

It was during the first postglacial period, 10,000 years ago, that the thick sheet of glacial ice slowly melted. The numerous glaciers locked in the valleys between the Vancouver Island mountain peaks scoured these same valleys and created the many lakes which pocket Vancouver Island. As they slowly receded over the east coast mountain slopes of Vancouver Island they deposited much glacial till. This material forms the bulk of the gravel in the Island's approximately 150 salmonid rivers and 200 plus named salmonid-bearing creeks.

The Oyster River watershed, including Adrian Creek, Woodhus Creek, and portions of the Little Oyster River, is accessible by MacMillan Bloedel logging roads which network throughout the upper valley and branch upwards following the many valleys of the eastern slopes of Mt. Alexandra & Mt. Adrian. Piggot Creek canyon and headwaters including the watershed of Harris Creek, a major tributary of Piggot Creek, are accessible by following the Timberwest Logging Company Oyster River mainline or Rossiter mainline. Both logging companies have a liberal public access policy but it is restricted to weekends or after working hours and is dependent upon fire hazard conditions.

For some of the Oyster River tributaries, Woodhus Creek and the Little Oyster River, this glacial till gravel has been at the heart of large salmonid nurseries. But, the Oyster River watershed has been greatly effected by forest removal. It has resulted in high floods with much of the gravel being washed downstream. As well, streambank clearcuts and road construction have resulted in heavy deposits of silt entering the river. This silt had left the remaining gravel as a deadly trap for salmon eggs, alevins and overwintering fry. Currently, high altitude tributaries in the Adrian Creek valley and throughout Piggot Creek are seeing their forest cover removed with the result that it will be many years before this watershed is once again stable. As well, current development on the Mt. Washington ski village area has resulted in numerous pollutants entering Piggot Creek and infecting the lower half of the Oyster River. But, these past insensitive actions in headwater areas have created a public awareness and ensured a future measure of protection for this beautiful watershed.

The Oyster River is the ideal winter steelhead stream for both the novice and the Fishhawk. Throughout its waters it provides ideal conditions for drift-fishing, float-fishing, fly-fishing, and combination fishing. It also offers bonus sea-run cutthroat trout, the result of a major provincial enhancement program. This latter program, started in the mid-1980s, is aimed at enhancement of sea-run cutthroat trout in the river and in the estuary area. Sea-run cutthroat trout are available throughout the river during all months of the year but concentrations appear at the estuary from April through September. The program has been highly successful and annually draws anglers from throughout the north-west.

A new fishery, estuary fishing for pink salmon, has become a highly popular sports fishery during August and early September. Enhancement of this species has provided annual runs of over 30,000 pink salmon to the river. These fish concentrate in the estuary area and are eagerly sought after by fly-fishermen using small flies like the pink eve fly pattern.

The Oyster River is a typical Vancouver Island run-off stream with well over half of its thirty miles in deep canyon stretches. The lower twelve miles of this mid-sized stream extends through a semi-accessible canyon which eventually opens to a broad floods plain in its lower half with multiple pools and deep green holding slots. Like all run-off streams, the Oyster has very low water conditions during late summer and very high flows during the late spring. The major runs of winter steelhead come prior to or during the early part of the high flows. Almost all run-off streams have an additional run of steelhead in late October and early November. These powerful fish are dubbed by old-timers as "fall fish." These are not summer-run steelhead but rather, a very early run of winter steelhead which begin their entry to their natal river during seasonal mid fall rains.

In the Oyster, these fall fish usually enter the river during the latter week of October and are available to steelheaders throughout the early weeks of November. December brings the next period of migrating fish in the Oyster but this is usually a small "Christmas" run. January and February also have small runs completely dependent upon water conditions and rain. Mid-March through to the end of April is the key angling period for the Oyster River. At this time, migrating fish are continually entering the stream in low and high water conditions with every change of tide. Late April sees these runs diminishing with fewer and fewer fish entering the river through to early June. Steelhead angling ceases when the high flows come from late spring melt on the high Forbidden Plateau.

The Oyster is a continually changing stream in its lower and middle reaches. These changes are the true challenge for the angler who annually fishes this stream.

The lower section of the river has multiple pools which are well defined and easy to fish. Experienced steelheaders realize that pools are resting places for fish on their spawning migration and that only a few have the very specific requirements demanded by steelhead as holding water. On the lower Oyster there are a multitude of pools but as usual only a very few are true holding water. Many of the pools and runs appear ideal and do hold an occasional resting fish but steelheaders will often spend far too much time on these to the exclusion of the major holding pools.

The middle section of the Oyster River extends from the Little Oyster Pool upstream to the entrance of the first canyon at Woodhus creek. This middle section is punctuated with exciting pools, runs, and holding riffles. It can be frustrating for the angler since this is the water where the fish continue to move. One day the stream will appear loaded with fish while during the next the fish will all appear to have left. This middle section runs through a wide plain surrounded by a bench on either side. The plain is composed primarily of poplar and alder forests opened periodically by meadows and small second-growth evergreen parks. The river is centered in a wide gravel bed stretching out on either side of the flowing water. It is truly an ideal stream for the fly-fisherman, having many gravel runs and pockets as well as many pools ideally suited for holding water. Open river-banks allow for long back casts and riffle water leading into pools acts as prime holding water. Occasionally clay banks and sandstone pockets provide specific permanent pools while loose dirt banks and wide gravel beds create new holding water annually.

The upper section of the stream provides the greatest challenge to the angler for it is here that the fish congregate. It is a difficult section to fish requiring cliff trips and deep pool fishing. In the canyon, sandstone and shale predominate, making the pools permanent. This has the advantage that once a pool is discovered it becomes a permanent targeted fish holt for the angler. However, the length of the canyon mitigates against consistent catches in those pools and makes angling in the canyon water a constant search for the fish. It is interesting to note that I have a number of key holding slots in these canyon waters which have annually held fish in the same identical location.

The sad and alarming recent decline of steelhead in the Oyster can be attributed to an increasing number of man-caused environmental disasters. These land-use problems are common to all coastal streams and are mentioned here in the hope that what has happened on the Oyster River can be avoided on other streams.

The most serious problem for all salmonids in the river has been the heavy damage to the river gravel from upstream logging which has resulted in tons of silt being deposited in the stream. As well as choking fish spawn, this silt has eliminated much of the aquatic life upon which the juvenile steelhead feed. As mentioned earlier, insen-sitive logging and poor road construction have also stripped stream-bank vegetation and caused the Oyster to become a yo-yo stream with sudden high flows scouring streambanks and shifting spawning gravel.

At the estuary and in the first mile of the river, channelization has virtually destroyed the numerous fishing pools and hold-rearing water which once made the Oyster famous as a steelhead stream. This downstream channelization has also resulted in extensive changes upstream, altering the course of the river and eliminating many smaller holding pockets.

Subdivision development along the lower river and upstream for about six miles has caused loss of access for anglers and serious water quality problems. Development of the Mount Washington ski hill has seriously polluted Piggot Creek adding numerous contaminants to this tributary with the result that now, downstream, extensive algae growth occurs. In the future water may also be diverted from the upper Oyster for agricultural and domestic uses. Unless legislation is enacted which will guarantee a minimum flow during the low water periods in summer and winter this will have a disastrous effect on salmonid production in this idyllic stream.

My associations with the Oyster have been numerous throughout the years. In previous paragraphs I have detailed many of the recent threatening actions which will undoubtedly have a long term effect on the river. Throughout this book, however, I do speak of many of my memorable and positive steelheading experiences. But, in this chapter it is my hope that the reader will take up the cause of the river and that future generations will have the opportunity to share wondrous angling experiences on this classical steelheading stream.

Puntledge River

Of all the rivers on Vancouver Island, the Puntledge River represents the death of an angler's dream. At one time equal to the greatest of the mainland streams and acknowledged in angling literature of the first half of the century as the stream to fish on Vancouver Island, the Puntledge today is but a sad reminder of what once was a truly outstanding sports fishing river. The Puntledge was once the nursery of Comox Bay's world-renowned tyee salmon where fish in the fifty-, sixty-, and even seventy-pound class were caught daily. Today, sadly, even Comox Bay must be closed to protect the very few remaining spawning adult chinook salmon. Once, the Puntledge was ranked among the top steelhead streams in British Columbia. Today, it is ranked as one of the lowest. As I write this, a total angling closure has been placed on the river to protect the three summer steelhead, all that were located in the river and likely the less than ten remaining from a once abundant race.

What was the disaster that virtually destroyed salmonid production in the vast headwater areas? The answer is likely B.C. Hydro's construction of a dam and power house in the 1950s, two deadly hazards which effectively blocked spawning and downstream migration. Other factors: the loss of spawning gravel, recent deadly predation by harbor seals, and overfishing have certainly contributed and are likely the main reasons there has been such poor rehabilitation success on the river.

I have many memories of steelheading on the Puntledge for I fished this stream in the late sixties and seventies before the drastic downturn of steelhead numbers occurred. It was at the Power House pool in 1965 that I beached my second steelhead. It was on that successful trip that my habits as an Interior rainbow fly-fisherman were literally sliced from my hand. As I wrote earlier, I was using an unfamiliar spinning reel and had cast to the center run on that late December morning. When the float suddenly disappeared, my patient steelheading partner yelled, "Strike!" I instinctively gripped the line in my index finger, lifted the rod to set the hook and began to strip monofilament line with my left hand. There was a sudden jolt on the rod and a large roiling surface steelhead began to strip nylon line through my fingers at a speed I had never experienced before— even with my larger Okanagan rainbow trout. Before I could react, the line had cut through my right palm and index finger and snapped when I was unable to give it sufficient slack. Since then, even though I have learned the art of strip casting for steelhead in difficult situations, I have always left the line in a position to play out of the rod guides with little interference on the initial run until I can gain control and fight the fish from the reel.

I have many special angling memories of the Puntledge. Many of these focus on a Friday afternoon Outdoor Club where I took twelve-year-old boys and girls to the river after school. Our success on those trips was limited but it seemed every second week one of the youngsters would hook into a water-walking trophy. These Friday afternoon trips were learning experiences for us all in the world's greatest classroom, the outdoors!

I also clearly recall one February morning when, as the tide receded, my partner and I figured that fresh-run steelhead would hold at the head of the highest point of tidal affect in the river, a location directly below the Condensory Bridge Pool. We began to fish this shallow run during high slack on that day waiting as the tide began to recede. Soon the run, which was a deep pool at high tide, began to show as the tide affect moved downstream. In moments we had an incredible matching twelve-pound double on. These were powerful fish and fought as titans, upstream to the bridge and, then, downstream to the distant meathole. Back at the run my partner hooked two other fish which he lost in rapid fashion as they bolted downstream. Then, again, a second double, a ten-and an eight-pounder which also fought in incredible fashion until they were finally beached. In the Puntledge and other rivers, I have since worked the tidal runs at virtually any time of the day with good success. But the memories of that first success are still firmly imprinted.

In recent years as trial enhancement programs have occurred on the river, I have been fortunate to be involved in many catch-for-hatchery programs with winter fish. I have learned that the Puntledge still holds a fair run of winter steelhead, introduced Quinsam River stock, who are particularly interested in flies. In these years the Puntledge has taught me to concentrate on white water slots for these are the areas where these fish prefer to hold.

These new winter fish seem to start to enter the river during late December. There is the usual slowing of fish entering during January and February and then the major concentration of winter steelhead enters late in March and early April.

A major hatchery facility has been constructed on the Puntledge River by the Federal Department of Fisheries. Steelhead enhancement has been minor but federal and provincial cooperation has occurred in an attempt to support these fish. Sadly, 700 plus harbour seals now reside in Comox Bay with about fifty of these actively entering the Puntledge to feed on adult salmon and steelhead. In the spring when salmonid smolts are migrating downstream, these river seals decimate smolt populations feeding voraciously on the compact groups of small fish. The seal predation problem is seen as political and it appears that no politician has the intestinal fortitude to provide the necessary seal harvesting solution to protect the Puntledge steelhead and salmon.

During the years of the Puntledge Hatchery, tragedy has struck on a number of occasions when thousands of steelhead fry have died

141

because water temperatures have risen to lethal heights. There can be no excuse for this obvious disregard for these fish.

But, I like to think and hope that times have changed. Fish, particularly salmonids, are important and we are seeing programs which hopefully will address the dire needs of this classic angling stream.

Quinsam River

Early one December, glowing reports about many steelhead being taken on the Campbell River below the confluence of the Quinsam and more guarded comments about bonanza catches from the Quinsam prompted me to organize a trip to the Quinsam with two of my steelheading partners. A forecast of six inches of new snow over the already heavy blanket covering the Campbell River area was no deterrent. We planned to fish separate waters at first light and then work together on the section above the old Argonaut bridge.

At daybreak I dropped one partner at the mouth of the Quinsam, a mile from the community of Campbellton on the Gold River Highway. I then backtracked to Quinsam Road and followed this past the rifle range to the Corner pool at the top of the government campsite and dropped off my other partner. I then drove upstream to the then abandoned Argonaut bridge, parked and was soon casting my float and terminal tackle in the Forestry Pool in full daylight.

The Quinsam River, the Campbell's major tributary, has one of the Island's most impressive runs of early big winter steelhead. Annually, there are a number of these fish taken in the over-twenty-pound class. Lunkers over twelve pounds are common and it was for these first of the season, bright, pinking Quinsam steelhead that we were searching. The males in this early run are quite distinct from later runs because of their pink mauve metallic shade. Only in later April and May does the distinctive pink again become common.

Moving downstream from the Forestry Pool, I float fished changing from roe to Gooey-bobs and then to Spin-and-Glo lures. The contrast of the red float top against the snow on the far bank had

142

an almost mystical effect on the early morning water. However, no movement below the water activated the drifting float during that first hour. When I finally met my partners downstream, one chattered brightly about a pinking twelve-pound buck that he had beached from the first pool in the campsite. Later, upstream, I talked with two anglers who had rolled two fish but were unable to hold them. "You should have been here last weekend!" was their parting comment after they told me of their outstanding success late in November.

My partners forged ahead along the angler's trail breaking a rough path through the thigh high snow to the confluence of Cold Creek, the current site of the Federal government fish hatchery. I followed them upstream past the famed Pipe Pool and finally stopped at the Alder Pool. Here, a gnarled and ancient fallen alder had effectively cut the pool in two and restricted fishing on this usually very productive run. The right color, the right flow, and nostalgic memories made the pool too tantalizing to leave even though many fresh wader tracks indicated that it had been well fished that morning.

With ever increasing casts, I slowly began to work the drift of the float across the river. When the float was almost ducking under the weeping branches on the far side, it abruptly disappeared. I struck fast but was dumbfounded by the geyser that burst from the water as a bright pinking sixteen-pound buck steelhead thrashed on the surface and then headed for the submerged alder. Snubbing down on the screaming Silex reel, I brought him to the surface. He made a spectacular leap and then changed direction. For ten minutes he flashed upstream and down until I finally eased him into the snowbank on the river's edge. Masses of scars crisscrossed his streamlined body telling of a mighty struggle somewhere in the Pacific Ocean. A split tail and deep scars on the wrist also told of a panic-filled flight from a seal.

Later, I cast again to the far side letting my Silex reel ease the float downstream near the overhanging alders. The float dipped quite suddenly and then surfaced before I had time to strike. Certainly another fish, but one which appeared hook-shy. The same slight take came again and again as I continued through that holt. Then, just as

143

sudden as the dip of the float, it was "Fish On!" as a prime eight-pound doe roiled the waters.

The superb actions of this hen put the larger buck to shame as she danced along the surface, whirled through the overhanging alders, leaped, tossed her head, and put a strain on both rod and reel unlike any I had experienced for a long time.

Upstream, one partner had a similar experience with two fish in another pool and finally managed to beach one weighing ten pounds. When we had at long last bushwhacked through the snow to the car, we tallied seven fish hooked and four beached. This is the Quinsam!

The construction of the Quinsam Salmon Hatchery in the lower reaches of the river has brought dramatic changes. Facilities for steelhead hatchery production have resulted in major increases in steelhead populations in the river. This has greatly increased angling pressure and eliminated the wild aspect of river angling. The development of the provincial campground in the lower mile and the construction of nature trails along the river's edge have had a positive effect by increasing the use of this river for uses other than angling. While these developments may appear an intrusion to the steelheader they have in fact ensured future protection and assured future access.

The Quinsam does have a historic run of summer steelhead which should be considered in hatchery production. There are miles of meandering waters accessible to the adventurous angler which could once again produce an exciting summer race. Summer steelhead should be given priority, like the Tsitika summer fish in the Campbell, if we are to perpetuate a unique sports fishery.

Salmon River

Vancouver Island's trophy steelhead stream!

Ask any steelheader where to go on Vancouver Island for trophy steelhead and the answer will always be, "Fish the Salmon River."

This past season while steelheading on the Salmon with my lifelong friend, Lew Carswell and his daughter, Leian, we were fortunate to see one more example of these Salmon River giants. Lew had been drift-fishing a deep, wide crescent run when he hooked this leviathan. It was not a flashy steelhead, one that surface walked then punctuated this wild activity with mad dashes around the pool, but, rather a heavy, dogged steelhead that took many minutes to bring to surface near the beach. When we were able to see the exposed tip of the tail and then the length, there was no doubt that this was one of those legendary fish.

I have beached thousands of steelhead from Vancouver Island streams as has Lew, whose job during the winter is to hook wild steelhead for the Fish and Wildlife Branch's hatchery program, but neither of us had ever seen an Island steelhead of this size! When it was finally near the shore the wrist near the tail was just too big to grip. The large dorsal hump magnified the immense size of what we both estimated was a steelhead well over thirty pounds in weight!

The Salmon is one of the larger river systems on Vancouver Island, feeding from all points of the massive Sayward forest. Access to the major portions of the river is limited, being restricted to the Salmon River Mainline logging road, the Island Highway and inland Menzie's Bay logging roads. In recent years, due to a management upstream angling closure above Big Tree Creek for much of the winter season, only the lower reaches of this river have been fished consistently. However, come the opening of the upper waters in mid-March, the area immediately below the confluence of the Memekay and the Salmon becomes the major winter steelhead fishing waters. In this area, and downstream, we are witness to the terrible results of streambank logging. Wide scoured gravel banks, sunken trees and logs, and ever shifting pools are a mausoleum to earlier unilateral logging practices in the Sayward forest.

In the Salmon, during late February, March, and April, runs of large steelhead with many reaching the trophy fifteen-to twenty-plus-pound class enter the river providing unsurpassed stream sport for the angler. Many deep runs but a limited number of pools provide holding water for these upstream migrating steelhead. Stumps and logging slash are common throughout these lower reaches with the result that steelheaders must be prepared for these hazardous and hidden snags when they play these large powerful fish.

Whenever I fish the Salmon River I am lured to the coffee shop at the White River auto court to gaze at the twenty-eight pound mounted steelhead framed on the wall. It is a steelhead the likes of which I had never seen taken from Vancouver Island waters until this last season. Earlier outdoor writers had written stories of these heavy trophies alluding to the fact that they held in the reaches of the river near the log and stump glutted pools below the confluence of the Memekay and Salmon rivers. It was in this area that I concentrated my earlier steelheading, mastering the steelhead holding water between the Memekay, Big Tree Creek, the Log Jam, and the White River. This is big water, yet because of the unstable river banks, the river predictably changed after every flood and there was the excitement of learning new water and locating new steelhead lies. But, always, there is the image of that gigantic steelhead mounted in the coffee shop. It brought me back again and again to this superb steelhead river in a search for these legendary giants.

My early steelheading on the Salmon River was one of the challenge of big water. The Salmon is a massive river for Vancouver Island, draining the immense Sayward forest between Campbell River and Kelsey Bay. It is fed by numerous tributaries from the high Vancouver Island Mountain Range and is joined by such tributary rivers as the South Fork of the Salmon, the Memekay River, and the White River. It is not a wading river although wide sand riffles can be crossed, carefully.

Two major tributaries and multiple minor creeks drain the Sayward Forest-Salmon River watershed. Then two major river tributaries, the Memekay and White, are also well-known steelhead streams; the Memekay for good winter steelheading and the White for an outstanding summer run. Big Tree Creek, a relatively minor tributary flowing into the Salmon once held surprisingly good steelheading during high flows. At one time it was not uncommon during low-water periods in March to spot steelhead in the very clear pools waiting for a change in water flows to continue thair spawning migration. A sheer falls directly below the Island Highway bridge crossing Big Tree Creek is the limit of upstream migration. Downstream, waters to the Salmon once provided approximately three miles of stream angling.

Unfortunately, like the other major streams flowing on the outskirts of the Campbell Lakes and the Elk Fall hydro power station, upstream waters on the Salmon have been diverted to fill the Campbell Lakes reservoir for the power station. "Power for Progress," has seriously crippled many Island streams and been the death of many major trout and salmon runs.

The Salmon River has received increased attention in recent years, a recognition of the fisheries resource potential of this large Vancouver Island stream. After the removal of the cedar canyon plug which blocked upstream access for adult fish to the vast upper watershed nursery, the Vancouver Island Fisheries Branch placed the Salmon River on an intensive steelhead rehabilitation program. Cooperation from B.C. Hydro, MacMillan Bloedel, the major forestry company harvesting timber in the watershed, and the Federal Department of Fisheries, has resulted in a number of major projects being conducted in the river and its watershed. All agencies have done extensive inventory of water, lands, forests, and fish. A hydro diversion dam which once drained a large portion of the river during low summer flows has been upgraded and more waters are now flowing through the river. An adult fishway, built to bypass the B.C. Hydro dam, was completed by the Department of Fisheries and Oceans in 1992. Monitoring of this diversion has shown a yearly increase in steelhead passage. Steelhead seeding of many upper tributaries is an ongoing project that will greatly enhance the river's future potential. Tributary creeks have been fertilized and a hatchery steelhead-fry-release program has been in effect for a number of years. This watershed cooperation has done much for the steelhead. Now that the cedar plug has been pulled in the lower river, these projects, in cooperation and with mitigation with industry, are leading to the revival of this majestic river. Continued fisheries effort, forest and water stewardship, and the ever-present angler guardians should ensure an increasing number of these legendary giants on the Salmon River.

Watch the Salmon River, it is Vancouver Island's steelhead sleeper!

Stamp River

It was late one August when I first fished the Stamp River. It was a time prior to the successful rehabilitation of salmon and steelhead by the Federal Department of Fisheries & Oceans and the Provincial Fish & Wildlife Branch at the Robertson Creek Hatchery facility. Yes, we found fish then, not many, but sufficient to draw me back every year since.

If I were to choose a Vancouver Island river which was my mentor through my early seasons of steelhead fly-fishing it would have to be the Stamp River. It is the Grassy Banks Run, immediately upstream of the famous General Noel Money Pool, which holds special memories for me of hooked summer and, more recently, winter steelhead.

Not too many years ago the Ash River entered the Stamp River immediately upstream of Money's Pool and below the Grassy Banks Run. Today, however, the Ash River, after breaking through an alder brake during a high flood a few years ago, enters the Stamp River half a kilometer upstream. But, it is that old entrance, now a wide backeddy, which provides outstanding holding water for all salmon migrating upstream to spawn.

Sitting on the big log beside the Grassy Banks Run provides an excellent view into the stream. I have often seen steelhead holding at the near shore immediately above the pool created by the old mouth of the Ash River. This is obviously tailout water and, as I have learned in so many Island rivers, it is the tailout which holds the majority of fish!

My favorite approach for fly-fishing this pool is to start casting while I am still on the grassy bank, letting my fly drift through the near water as I move downstream. Walking back upstream, I will then wade into the Grassy Banks Run (be warned, it is fast water!) and move downstream while I work a dead drift fly through the water as far out as mid stream. It is while I am approaching the tailout that I begin to tense, for it is here that the majority of fish have taken my flies. If the river flow is low, I have found that I can move downstream almost to the gravel drop-off into the Old Ash Pool. This is prime holding water and needs to be covered thoroughly and with many repeated casts to the same area to be certain that you have tempted all the catchable steelhead which will be holding in this water. Be warned, though, not to walk downstream too far! On a number of occasions I have found that I have done just that and, due to the force of the current, I have been unable to push my way upstream against the force of the water. Only a partner or my third leg, a wading staff, have saved me from swimming in the river.

The far side of the Old Ash Pool is a prime holding run of water for steelhead. It is accessible to the wading steelheader in the summer, but only at extreme casting range. The winter steelheader needs a boat to reach this water due to the higher river flows.

Drift boats and jet boats are a recent intrusion on the Stamp, particularly in those lower waters which enter the Somass. I have heard it said that jet boats have a positive influence for the beach angler because as they pass over waters where steelhead lie they will shift the fish into areas more accessible to the beach-wading angler. They will also keep the fish moving in a stream, making them more accessible to all anglers. Possibly there is some truth in this, but my experiences with jet boats have all been frustrating. One particular incident soured a day's angling when, while wading on one particularly productive stretch of water, a jet boat roared upstream, under my drifting float and anchored in mid stream such that I could no longer drift the run properly. The question of allowing jet boats for steelheading needs to be addressed such that only certain sections of rivers should be open for their use. The time is ripe for specific site regulations on all our rivers. Like fly-only water, jet boat access must be restricted.

In recent years, I have spent many hours on the enhanced Stamp and upper Somass Rivers. The Somass is formed where the Stamp and the Sproat Rivers join. Many steelheaders refer to the mile length below the confluence of these two rivers as "the magic mile." Judging from the number of steelhead I have hooked in this section, it is well named. The reason for this affluence of fish is likely the fact that it is here that most steelhead smolts were released; hence, their homing on their return spawning migration has been to this section of the river.

Other sections of the Stamp River also produce good winter and now good summer steelheading. Certainly one productive pool lies at the foot of Stamp Falls. It is one of the elbow-to-elbow sections of the river but it does provide outstanding steelheading. Another major section is the Money's Pool area, a long wide crescent run with large kidney stone boulders at the tailout of the pool which seem to hold many fish. Money's Pool stretches about a half mile below the Grassy Banks Run and is likely the most fished stretch of steelheading water on Vancouver Island.

There are many prime fly-fishing pools on Vancouver Island's 200 plus steelhead streams and creeks. But, there are few pools like the Stamp River's Grassy Banks Run and Old Ash Pool and few rivers like the Stamp and the Somass that offer so many opportunities for both summer and winter steelhead fly-fishing!

White River

For the fifth time the float drifted by the rock wall, then shot underwater as the finicky summer run steelhead snatched at the bait offering. But, this time the hook struck home and in moments the fish was throwing rainbow spray in the sunlight of that precipitous canyon pool.

The fly sank quickly in the foaming water and then just as it began to arc across the stream; a sudden halt—a strike, then a golden sea-run cutthroat trout catapulted in a tireless run through the sparkling water.

The Spin-and-Glo lure had barely touched the water when the line tightened and a big fish streaked along the surface, its dorsal fin knifing the water as it sought to escape. When finally beached, its obvious forked tail proved it to be a coho even though this was only the first day of August.

Breaking through the dense pristine hemlock stand along the riverbank elk trail, I stood on the edge of a salmonberry—devil's club meadow. The heavy musky odor of elk floated throughout. Numerous beds in the tall grass beside the bogs plus fresh tracks which led across the river showed that we had been "that" close.

Later, stopping by the edge of yet another elk wallow, I picked up a fallen antler dropped by some magnificent bull last winter.

Breaking through a thick patch of devil's club, I finally stepped on the beach of the most beautiful river pool I had ever seen. The water was crystal clear although a dark shadow spread from the head of this wide crescent pool almost to the tailout. After viewing the sheer beauty of this hidden gem, I stepped forward to start fishing at the head of the pool. It was then that this shadow carpet suddenly moved shifting in tandem to the other side of the pool. I was astounded! Here were steelhead and coho salmon in uncountable numbers!

All these are memories eternal for the outdoorsman who has had the privilege and rare fortune of being one of the first to sample the treasures of an unexploited wilderness watershed headwater.

The White River is located almost in the geographic center of Vancouver Island, in the heart of the towering Sutton Mountain Range. Mount Victoria (7,095 ft), the second highest mountain on Vancouver Island, splits the White from its major tributary, Concert Creek, whose headwaters in Stewart Lake are overlooked by Queens Peak. The upper White, once a meandering system of pristine elk meadows and salmonid nurseries, is fed by the sheer alpine heights of the Sutton mountains and eventually leads through the White-Gold Pass to the headwaters of the Gold River.

Its location, plus the anomaly of having its flood plain in the upper watershed and a fifteen-mile-long canyon in its lower reaches, protected the White Valley from exploitation until the 1970s. Today, a major logging road has breached this canyon and clearcut logging scars mark the insensitive exploitation of this valley. Sadly, the company's logging plans will strip the valley bottom and take all marketable timber through to the river's edge.

Today, the memories of anglers searching for the wild, untouched beauty of nature are being overlaid with scenes of silt-laden waters oozing through to the river from violated nursery tributaries; and, of the gouged landscape laid naked from clearcut logging; and, of jungles of carelessly discarded slash blocking the once tranquil and adventurous elk trails; and, of coho fry exposed in the open-slash sloughs, darting to escape the sudden shadows we cast across the debris clogged creeks; and, of a riverbank stripped to a single tree every fifty feet, ripe for scouring and erosion during the fall and spring run-offs and freshets; and, of trees cut along the riverbank, eventually to wash downstream scouring spawning gravel beds; and, of alders along the riverbank and tributaries, lifeless and rotting, victims of intentional hack-and-squirt poisons; and, of logging road-bed gravel dug from the redds of spawning fish.

The concerns of sportsmen and naturalists for the outstanding natural features of this unique river valley led organized groups throughout the province to petition for measures of protection. The measures requested would guarantee a green strip suitable for the protection of the river, its tributary streams, creeks, and elk meadows. These areas are vital for the rearing of salmonid fishes and are used extensively by elk, deer and other wildlife for food and shelter. Unfortunately, today, as I now tour the river valley along company logging roads, I am saddened by what has come to be. Clearcutting still occurs, streambanks are still denuded and little appears to have been done to protect and enhance the special fish and wildlife in this watershed.

On a river swim to count salmonids, in August 1993, with members of the B.C. Fisheries Branch, I was elated to see two very large summer steelhead holding in a special canyon pool. Both fish placed in the sixteen-to twenty-pound range and brought back exciting memories of similar fish in earlier years. During our four mile swim we only counted seventeen steelhead, fifty-three summer coho and twenty-six Dolly Varden. This was a low count from the normal 100 plus steelhead and I can only hope the White will not follow the pattern of other Island rivers by slowly decreasing its numbers of these magnificent sports fish.

Five

Steelhead Management

Management Principles

The stream angler first experiencing the sport of steelheading is oblivious to all else in his obsession to beach a silver trophy. In time, however, he learns a little about the life history of his fish. He realizes that, unlike resident trout, they are not feeders and that he must learn to read the river's changes and conform to the habits of a migrating rainbow trout. His fish demands specialized tackle and techniques which further compounds and complicates his angling. At about this time he also becomes conscious of the river environment and of the needs and desires of other steelheaders. He comes to appreciate the wonders of the stream with its minute aquatic life and infinite terrestrial insects; the wild animals, birds, and plants; the changes in water temperature, color, and flow, all of which compact on his angling experience.

Steelhead management is similarly complex. I know that in this chapter I am only making a start on the broad area of steelhead management. However, like the novice angler who has eventually learned about specialized tackle and the skills of his sport, I have spent many years examining the complexity of the subject and now feel able to draw some conclusions.

Much has occurred in the management of British Columbia's steelhead since that eventful time in 1971 when the federal government fully relinquished its claim on this species and gave full authority and responsibility to the provincial Fisheries Branch of the Ministry of Environment, Lands & Forests for all freshwater management of steelhead. Angling effort has increased as has the annual catch of steelhead; the majority of B.C. rivers have been inventoried and catalogued for fish species and for steelhead habitat; angling habits have altered considerably with catch-and-release dominating the earlier catch-and-kill habits; management has been responsive to angler needs and, with the numbers of steelhead now available, there is no question that "the good old days are today!"

In the overall management of steelhead angling and conservation there are primary principles which must underline all specific management programs. These principles determine the very basis for the survival of the fish and the sport for those who pursue this most worthy trophy. Observance of these principles by those in decision-making capacities will determine the survival of a unique British Columbian way of life and a unique life species.

Management Principles

1. **The highest priority for steelhead management must always be for wild stocks.**

The greatest feature of the steelhead resource in British Columbia is the variability and viability of its wild stocks. Today, every stream with indigenous populations of steelhead finds itself with an almost infinite variety. In many there are both summer-run and winter-run fish, both distinctive races with their variabilities. If we examine just one race, the winter-run steelhead which is the most common, we find that in any given river adult fish will return to their home river and tributary to spawn beginning sometime late in November and continuing through until May. At certain times during this return to their natal river there will be peak runs where large numbers of fish will enter the river in varying stages of spawning ripeness. These specific runs are distinct and definitive to that particular river and often to that specific section of the river. Nature's preservation of these runs is ensured by the spawning differences of these fish in the event that some natural river catastrophe occurs which may destroy the eggs of early or late spawners.

Steelhead, unlike salmon, do not die following the spawning act. The second-time spawners are the insurance that the run is perpetuated should any natural disaster occur which might destroy the eggs or fry of the first-time spawners.

As fry and adults one further variable exists which also ensures that a specific run will be perpetuated. This is the late-maturing factor which will see fry staying in a stream longer than the usual two years. In some cases fry will remain for three, four and even five years before they smolt. This same late maturing factor also occurs in the ocean. The usual stay in the ocean is for two years. But, some fish, the true lunker trophy steelhead which will reach the eight-plus kilogram class, will stay in the ocean for up to five years.

In sum, the factors of river entry, spawning ripeness, second spawning, and variable maturity provide for numerous combinations which will ensure the return and perpetuation of steelhead to their home river. These are our wild fish!

Should managers consider any other option than the preservation and perpetuation of this variability and viability, then the steelhead and the steelhead angler will be the losers. Steelhead in every river are unique and have evolved site specific to that peculiar stream. In actual fact in each river they have become a distinct race and should be classified according to their home river. We should have a Gold River steelhead, a Cowichan River steelhead, a Thompson River steelhead, and so on. To take one race and plant it in another river with an indigenous race would create a bastard race, genetically polluted and unable in the long term to cope with the specifics of that particular stream. Should it be necessary to use artificial rearing techniques in any river they must only be done with brood stock native to the stream to be rehabilitated. In this way we will ensure the perpetuation of our wild stocks.

In rivers where steelhead have declined dramatically, now is the time to preserve the wild stock before a river race becomes extinct! Salmonid gene banks must be established to preserve the viability and variability of steelhead stocks. Cryopreservation of sperm (that is, preservation in a frozen state) from males captured during brood fishing is now possible. The facility is available and "in place." All rivers where declines indicate a serious threat to that race should be a part of the salmonid gene bank.

2. **Steelhead must be legally recognized as the classic British Columbian trophy freshwater sports fish. Legislation must be enacted which will remove steelhead from all commercial categories.**

It is hard to conceive that this is not already the case for, eventually, anyone who spends any time fishing in B.C. freshwater will find that angler talk will turn to the supreme sporting qualities of steelhead caught in fast-flowing streams. Steelhead are in fact the measure of the experience! Its elusive nature and limited numbers, coupled with its size and the pristine environment in which it is sought, has marked the steelhead in the eyes and hearts of B.C. anglers as the ultimate freshwater sports fish. However, what has evolved as a social fact in the angling fraternity is not fact in law. Current legislation does not show this recognition and the steelhead is lumped with other game fish in regulations.

Legislation giving steelhead "trophy" status is an absolute if we are to eliminate the present commercialization of these supreme quality sports fish by industry and thoughtless anglers. Legislated trophy status would make it illegal for these fish to be caught and kept by any commercial means. Ironically, steelhead, now a commercial salmon species in B.C., are not considered a necessary fishery by the industry. In fact, in 1991 the commercial catch of steelhead was twenty-six tonnes compared to all salmon which was 85,680 tonnes or .0003 percent of the coastwide salmon catch. Sadly, if we look at this statistic, twenty-six metric tonnes equals 57,200 pounds or 8,171 steelhead. (The current average weight of steelhead has been estimated at seven pounds.) However, remember these are claimed or "landed" steelhead and do not constitute the thousands that we know are caught incidentally then counted with the sockeye, coho, and chum in the salmon net fisheries. Regulations necessary to protect steelhead would insist that salmon nets not be placed in major steelhead migration routes (Johnstone Strait, Lower Fraser, and Skeena rivers) and should steelhead be caught incidentally they will be resuscitated then released.

I would suggest that the time has come for the provincial government to recognize and acknowledge the social evolution of steelhead in our angling rich province and pass legislation which will make steelhead the official fish of the province of British Columbia. It is only fitting to add the steelhead, this special wildlife species which inhabits our vast water resources to the current B.C. Official Flower, the dogwood, and the B.C. Official Bird, the Steller's jay.

3. **Steelhead and other fish must have recognition as having rights to the water where they exist.**

Incredible as it may sound, nowhere in the B.C. Water Act is there recognition for fish as users of water. B.C. is known as a province which dams its rivers with careless regard to the needs of anadromous species of fish. In the past it has allowed the removal of critical river spawning gravel, road construction with careless abandon across spawning and nursery streams and the stripping of the vital greenbelt by industry and urban developers. As well, it provided other innumerable concessions to industry for the use of water.

It is imperative that legislation be enacted which guarantees that basic need of fish—water! This legislation must include protection in the form of guaranteed minimum flows and basic stream, streambank, and watershed protection.

4. **Preservation of streams and the steelheading experience demands an inviolate conservation belt of pristine or mature vegetation along both banks of all streams. This conservation belt should be defined and managed site-specific to the needs of each watershed.**

It is incredible that today the umbilical lifeline of every watershed, its protective greenbelt, is still open to every gross abuse of exploitation and development. Volumes have been written about the critical importance of stream bank vegetation to protect the water quality of streams. The conclusions in every report state emphatically that a strip of vegetation, a conservation belt, must be preserved to protect the integrity of the streams.

Specifically, a streambank greenbelt protects deciduous species, particularly alder which is the major contributor of nitrogen in the ecosystem of the watershed. It provides shade and shelter for fish and minimizes increases in water temperature. It acts as a filter to prevent sedimentation from entering the water system. It provides a buffer from overland run-off and acts as a catch basin against debris from this run-off water. It prevents direct solar radiation and protects the area from direct precipitation impact. It maintains adequate oxygen levels for all stream life. It provides the major food stuff or biomass for fish. It provides protective access for fish to their spawning grounds. It provides a profusion of plant growth, rich in nutrients for fish and wildlife. And, it preserves the aesthetic qualities desired by the stream angler.

To preserve the quality of water, the lifeblood of every watershed, it is imperative legislation be enacted in B.C. ensuring a conservation belt on both sides of rivers and their tributaries.

5. **Small streams with anadromous salmonids, whether tributaries of larger systems or complete watersheds, must receive the highest priority for environmental protection and steelhead enhancement.**

In recent years there has been a wellspring of recognition that in actual fact the river is but a highway for migrating adult steelhead. It is the small streams, the tributaries, and the upper headwaters that are the vital nurseries for steelhead, cutthroat trout, and coho salmon. Coupled with this recognition is also the fact that at one time virtually every small stream and creek with unhindered access to the sea once held a native population of steelhead. Unfortunately, because of the diminutive size of these creeks, industry has been brutal with these small nurseries. Also, because of their location, usually at points where human population growth occurs, urban development has been equally brutal with impassable culverts, roads, channelization, and other developments which have destroyed the unique races of steelhead in these nursery creeks.

Fortunately, in most cases these small systems are still capable of providing rearing habitat and in some cases very specific fisheries. Governments at all levels must insist upon protective measures for these small watersheds and incorporate covenants that will ensure no future destruction by industry or urban development will occur.

6. **Steelhead angling regulations must be watershed-specific and often stream-section specific. "Blanket management" should never be used.**

Much has changed in the management of the steelhead angler in the past few decades. The current regulations guide does provide "special notes" relating to various steelhead rivers. Yet, as one old world fly angler said to me on the riverbank one day, "People here (B.C.) do not have a feeling of ownership, a feeling of caring for their rivers. It is all the same whether I fish the Gold, the Cowichan, or the Stamp."

In the past, angler regulations have been based upon "blanket" policies. These are regulations which cover large regions with a single regulatory measure such as one fish per day from Region 6, an area encompassing a full quarter of the province. Blanket regulations are a bureaucratic utopia, particularly as they are managed from a central office far removed from the watershed. But, in the field, on the river, they are a nightmare.

We have come a long way in management regulations but we must strive to meet the goal that every watershed is a multifaceted, delicately balanced, exacting ecosystem that must be managed specific to its unique existence and potential.

7. **Public access to all B.C. watersheds must be an inherent right of all British Columbians.**

The problems of stream angler access are multiple and complex, including such issues as riparian rights, First Nations land claims, concessions to resource extraction industries, and private land ownership. The only solution which will ensure the preservation of steelhead angling is a Public Access Act. Simply put, this act would provide guaranteed access throughout a watershed including along streambanks, whether owned or controlled by private landowners, First Nations peoples, industry, or government. Included in this act would be those site specific restrictions necessary to preserve the special qualities and unique aspects of that watershed as well as its quality and integrity.

It is my firm belief that restrictive access policies during the midtwentieth century by the logging industry on Vancouver Island led to the loss of a summer run steelhead sports fishery on the east coast of Vancouver Island. It is a documented fact that the majority of the east coast streams held viable summer run populations but grotesque land abuse by logging companies eradicated these populations. Highly restrictive and, in most cases, no access ensured that the steelheader, the natural river guardian, was unaware of the potential fishery, the abuse, or the loss.

8. **Regulatory measures must always give priority to the B.C. resident steelheader. No regulation should ever eliminate angling opportunity for the B.C. resident.**

   Steelheading is a rare and unique Canadian angling sport originating in B.C. It has evolved as a specific B.C. heritage and must be preserved as such. Regulations which have specified certain trophy streams have recognized the priority of B.C. residents. In all future regulations this recognition must continue such that restrictions on B.C. steelheaders only occurs after all possible regulatory measures have been placed on non-residents.

   At no time should regulations ever take away the opportunity for steelhead angling. Steelhead entering streams on their upstream migration are incredibly hardy fish. When hooked and released they are known to fully recover within a day providing reasonable care has occurred during their release. Current catch-and-release regulations are applied as a recognition of the priority to preserve angling.

   Only when a river race is nearing extinction, such as that shown by the Puntledge River summer steelhead, must a closure then occur.

9. **The organized steelheader must be recognized as representing public opinion for present and future management of steelhead and the sport of steelhead angling.**

   Concern is often expressed at the political level and at the government agency level for the pressures of the "special interest group." Such has been the case against the organized steelheader. In fact it has even been suggested that the organized steelheader does not represent "public opinion." This is not so! Because of the very nature of the sport of steelheading, considerable personal contact is maintained between members and other anglers in the field where opinions and concerns are constantly being expressed. Because of the nature of steelheading, these concerns are funnelled to the organization and clubs which represent this sport. The organized steelheader does not have a vested interest in his demands as special interest groups often do.

161

Rather, as an organization, it is the marrying of incredibly diverse political, social, economic, and philosophic individuals to a common cause—the well being of another living species, the steelhead trout, and the environment where they and other species live. Managers must recognize these facts and take advantage of the experience, expertise, and organization of steelheaders.

Musings at Pool and Riffle

I have had the rare opportunity to have experienced the full spectrum of angling experiences with steelhead, from the exploration of pristine watersheds to the confines of a hatchery pool. All experiences have been unique and each has provided me with a perspective which either epitomizes the past or forecasts the future.

Yet, with all these experiences, it is the rivers which have remained most memorable. Unquestionably, in salmonid management, it is the river which must receive the highest priority. These are the watersheds of life! It is in the rivers that we have the salmonid's birthright: clean gravel percolated with unpolluted oxygenated water; a protective greenstrip of streambank vegetation providing prolific biomass; riffles and deep sheltered pools to harbor both young and adult fish alike. The future will measure and judge us by the state of our rivers and whether or not we have affected and effected the philosophy and policies acknowledging that a healthy river is a river with salmonids.

*   *   *

I am continually reminded by my angling friends that I must not tell that final detail—the where of each experience. Their good natured bantering takes on a much more serious form of intimidation when they realize it is a favorite river or location of their's of which I write.

While a columnist, this was the major criticism I had to face whenever I spoke with them or spoke to others of places they had been and successes they had had. It is with deep empathy that I can share their concern of the potential hoards which will descend when a specific location is permanently set in print.

My concern, however, takes an even more fundamental perspective, a simplicity of which I have occasionally been accused, but it is one which many years, many trips and many issues have crystallized. I fear for the survival of our sport of steelhead angling! Yes, fishing will be with us as long as we have water. But, the specifics of British Columbia steelheading, the social and historic traditions and mores which have grown with the sport during the twentieth century—it is these for which I fear.

Literature provides a measure of the human race at that precise historical time. It is this which must be expanded to ensure that the future knows from what base they work. When the present and the future have that precise base, then they will know what must be preserved and upon what they can afford to make concessions.

*   *   *

It is unfortunate that as steelhead populated new watersheds in their primordial migrations south along the North American coast of the Pacific Ocean, they did not change their color and shape to match each specific watershed they colonized. Truly this would have been fortunate for the modern steelheader and fisheries manager, for then they would recognize in a dramatic fashion the obvious fact that each watershed eventually evolved a distinct and separate race as decidedly different and unique as a steelhead.

The Commercial Slaughter

Steelheaders, do you know the value of that last trophy steelhead you caught? According to a 1991 report from DFO the actual price paid to commercial fishermen averaged $5.76 per steelhead; not $5.76 per ounce or $5.76 per pound but, $5.76 for each steelhead!!!

If we are to save our steelhead it is an absolute imperative they be decommercialized!

When the fifteen-plus-centimeter steelhead smolt reaches the salt water of the Pacific Ocean, following its two-to five-year nursery stay in stream and tributary headwaters, it begins an aquatic odyssey which will take it many thousands of miles.

Traveling at a little more than a kilometer per hour it will move to the outer coast of North America in the open North Pacific Ocean mingling with its near and distant relatives, summer and winter steelhead from other Pacific Northwest rivers and creeks, feeding on bait fish as it fully develops in its role as a primary predator of the aquatic ecosystem.

Much has been discovered about the migration of the North American and Asian steelhead in the water of the North Pacific Ocean in the past two decades. This has been documented in "Bulletin Number 51, 1992," of the International North Pacific Fisheries Commission, a document I would recommend highly to any who wish to know more about steelhead. Through international high seas tagging programs we now know that steelhead inhabit the open Pacific Ocean waters north along the North American continent to fifty-eight north latitude and, following a southerly swing with the Aleutian Island chain of Alaska, swim in waters as far east as 160 east longitude, thence south to the forty-second north latitude—an immense body of water.

However, it is in this formidable saline environment that the steelhead races are dealt a near fatal blow. Here they become a "non-target" salmon of the commercial net fishery and as such are the victims of a slaughter the magnitude of which has caused the destruction, the extinction, of whole river races.

I no longer feel that compromise which considers a commercial fishery for steelhead is possible if our trophy trout are to survive.

My proposal is one that organized steelheaders have voiced for the past quarter century. Provincial and federal governments, the Ministry of Fish, Wildlife & Parks and the Department of Fisheries and Oceans must make it illegal to land steelhead commercially. Making it illegal to have a steelhead on a commercial vessel places the onus on Fisheries and the commercial sector to find ways and/or new equipment which will be less likely to intercept steelhead in the same waters where commercial salmon fishing occurs.

The concept of the steelhead trout as a trophy fish is accepted in the U.S.A. in those western states with streams entering the Pacific Ocean: Washington, Oregon, California, and Idaho. In these states it is illegal for commercial net fishermen to retain steelhead caught incidentally by commercial fishing methods. They recognize the uniqueness of this member of the salmonid species and its sporting qualities.

Commercial fishing for steelhead in California was ended by legislation in 1924. In Washington State, commercial fishing for steelhead has been restricted to various Indian tribes on their reservations or at alternate sites when their traditional fishing areas are flooded after dam construction. In Oregon, commercial fishing for steelhead was restricted to the Columbia River in 1963. Further curtailment followed the declaration by the Oregon Legislature in 1969, that the steelhead was to be classed as a game fish. The Oregon classification recognizes that commercialization of steelhead debases the quality of this trophy sports fish. It also recognizes the economic importance of the species is in the sports creel rather than the commercial can.

In recent years much political attention has been focused on the efforts to protect the various steelhead races of the Skeena River. All this is well and good should it ever prove to be effective. However, what efforts are being applied for the rest of the province's steelhead rivers and unique individual steelhead runs?

J.C. Wightman, Senior Fisheries Biologist on Vancouver Island, highlighted in a report the following commercial fishery steelhead kill problems for Vancouver Island and adjacent mainland steelhead streams:

1. Interception of winter steelhead during late November and early December during "clean-up" fisheries for some east coast chum stocks such as the Nimpkish and Cowichan.

2. Interception of winter steelhead kelts taken in the net fisheries targeting June sockeye returns.

3. Interception of the summer-run steelhead maiden spawning populations during mixed stock fisheries on the Vancouver Island.

It should be noted that unlike salmon, more than 20 percent of spawning steelhead will recover from the trauma of the spawning run to spawn a second time. These four and five plus year fish are the elite of the population, being the strongest and the most adapted to survive. Their loss to a commercial fishery who dub them "snakes" because of their emaciated condition and low fat value is unforgivable to steelhead anglers.

In the past, it was fatalistically accepted by steelhead anglers that the majority of steelhead were dead if they were captured in the various commercial salmon net fisheries. Studies, however, have shown that this is not the case and that, in fact, there is a high survival rate in many cases. The determining factor for survival in the net is the length of time the net is left in the water by commercial fishermen. In one report the San Juan gillnet fleet had longer net sets, often five or six hours, and reported a six percent survival of steelhead, whereas, Fraser River gillnetters had shorter sets, usually one hour or less, and had an 80 percent survival of steelhead. This report also states that the survival in seine nets is "relatively high" with an 89 percent survival in the San Juan fishery. As one provincial fisheries biologist stated, "Clearly gillnet 'technology' is going to have to be replaced if we are at all serious about conservation, genetic integrity, bio-diversity, etc." Yes, steelhead can be thrown back in most cases when they have been caught by the commercial salmon fleet, with the expectation of a high survival rate!

Speaking with fisheries officers, I was enlightened with the manner in which steelhead are often counted in the commercial fleet. It appears that a technique called the "Hail Count" is used to determine the number of steelhead in each vessel. To achieve this "count," fisheries officers boat amongst the fleet and "hail" or call to the commercial boat asking, "How many steelhead today?" The commercial salmon vessel captain supposedly calls out the number he has in the boat which is then duly recorded by the fisheries officers. The officers then boat to the next commercial vessel and the process is repeated. Accurate—not in a "fish's eye"! It has been said by many that the number is less than a third of the "real" kill. Many fisheries officers feel the only way we can be certain of the real kill, the "by-catch," which is the new jargon, is to have an independent observer on board each gillnet or seine boat. A much simpler solution, say the organized steelheaders, would be to outlaw the commercial kill of steelhead coastwide!

One final sad note must be shared. In speaking with the Provincial Fisheries Branch about the steelhead data I have gathered, they corrected one factor I was going to use, the average size of steelhead. It appears that the average weight of steelhead has declined in the past two decades, averaging today at only seven pounds, down from the magic ten pounds of the 1970s. Reports do show that the average weight of steelhead taken in the commercial sector in the past was about twelve pounds.

Will we only have half-pounders or residual kokanee-like steelhead? Is this the future of our steelhead in the twenty-first century?

The time has certainly come for British Columbia to recognize the social and economic values of steelhead as a non-commercial species. Steelhead in a commercial can are an effrontery to the classic qualities of this unique world-renowned trophy trout! Steelhead must be classified as a trophy game species in British Columbia and given status to forever eliminate them as a by-catch from the commercial salmon fishery!

The Lake And Run-Off Theory

Conscientious steelhead anglers who have kept diaries realize that many Vancouver Island streams have a very early run of winter steelhead, some as early as October but, usually, in mid-November. These runs tend towards large fish and are the result of autumn rains which annually flood the rivers at this time. These fish are available to the ardent steelheader but success is usually limited.

These early fish are the forerunners of the large December runs which have traditionally opened the winter steelhead season on Boxing Day. This tradition has slowly ebbed during the past decade as steelhead anglers have become more mobile and as sizable runs now occur in hatchery supplemented rivers like the Stamp, the Nimpkish, the Campbell and Quinsam systems, the Little Qualicum, the Big Qualicum, the Englishman, and the Nanaimo.

The following pattern of steelhead run timing on Vancouver Island has proven itself over many of the years that I have been fortunate to angle for these trophy fish. If pursued by the novice or expert steelheader it is certain to increase his sport and catch.

On the east coast of the Island, lake fed streams have their major wild winter steelhead runs climaxing in late February and early March. Run-off streams, on the other hand, will tend to peak one month later, in late March and early April. It must be noted that hatchery augmented streams vary considerably in major run timing. These hatchery or "urban" steelhead, have been produced to supplement wild stocks. Their sheer numbers and artificial timing make it imperative that anglers fishing these streams for the first time gain local knowledge or information from the provincial Fisheries Branch.

Two major factors support the lake fed and run-off theory. First, lake-based streams are fed from waters which are warmer during the winter months with the result that temperature change will move the fish into the river system at this earlier time. Evolution, "nature's safety valve," accounts for the seemingly tardy migration in run-off streams. In run-off streams, late winter flash floods or freshets effectively scour the gravel and flush eggs from the redds. As a result, only the eggs of the later migrating fish survive to perpetuate the species. This theory is strengthened by the fact that lake fed streams tend to hold a specific flow. This holds true even during flood periods because of the capacity of the lake to act as a catch basin to ease the flow into the river.

West coast streams differ from the east coast of Vancouver Island because of topography. Canyon waters ease the flow and protect the gravel. West coast streams also support a competitive race of steelhead, the summer-run fish. This species extends the angling season but because of overlapping runs of winter and summer fish in April/May and October/November, it is difficult to theorize.

There are river systems which dispute this run-off and lake fed theory. One in particular, the Little Qualicum, will have runs peaking during the Christmas holidays and will continue peaking throughout the winter well into late April, even though it is a lake fed stream.

The Big Qualicum on the other hand fits the pattern exactly, as do most other east coast streams. For example, the Cowichan, the Puntledge, the Big Qualicum, and the Campbell, are all lake fed and peak late in February. Success is limited on these streams early in April. The Englishman, the Oyster, and the Salmon, are run-off streams and have their major runs late in March and early April. Success doesn't decline on these streams until late in April.

Without a doubt, the most important month for the winter steelheader is March. This is the month when the warming waters activate the stocks of fish which have moved into the river during the earlier winter months. This literal stockpile almost guarantees the angler a fish if he knows how to present his tackle.

December, on the other hand, may not have a stockpile of steelhead throughout the river but early runs in the lower reaches will account for many bonanza trips for the angler who logs river time. December is also known for its runs of big steelhead with fish in some systems, like the Nimpkish, Somass, and Campbell-Quinsam, reaching weights over twenty pounds.

December exploration and river time will make the angler aware of runs and pools for greater success later in the season. It will also ensure him some early trophy steelhead.

*　　　*　　　*

It has been the environmental issues, including habitat protection and species survival, which have made me realize what a precarious position now exists for our sport of steelheading. It seems that only when site-specific watersheds have received massive media coverage that minor concessions have been granted by industry or government. It has appeared that these slight appeasements have been sufficient for the lay public and hence have stemmed the tide of social and management revolution. But, are we so gullible that we will expect these minor concessions to ensure the survival of our sport? Industry, we know, has the 110 percent approach to their business while government agencies who carry out policy only have 60 to 80 percent staff and low budgets. Their approach, therefore, has to be towards the minimum. What remains for future generations? How can they have anything more than the minimum unless we intercede at all levels: at home, in our schools, in the media, in business, and in government agencies. What will be the legacy we will leave for the steelhead anglers of the twenty-first century?

The Urban Steelhead

In British Columbia there is a major factor which must be considered in the planning for the artificial propagation of steelhead. This concerns the dense population centers of the Lower Mainland and the east coast of Vancouver Island. The Fraser Valley accommodates one of the densest human settlements in North America. It and the population centers of the east coast of Vancouver Island are a fisheries management zone unique in British Columbia and must be managed as separate entities from the remainder of the province.

Fortunately, besides the Fraser River, which penetrates at least a third of the province, there are many coastal river systems which are complete and contained within this zone. It is on these latter systems that enlightened and progressive forms of steelhead management could occur.

The concept of the urban steelhead is the idea which has risen in response to the vocal demands of organized steelheaders who oppose wholesale and indiscriminate transplanting of steelhead stocks. Fortunately, the managers have responded positively by making wild steelhead the management priority throughout the province.

The urban steelhead is a hatchery steelhead raised for the sole purpose of providing sport in the densely populated centers of the province. Undoubtedly, it has provided the compromise necessary to satisfy the demands of the angling public in river systems near dense population centers. But, the development of the urban steelhead must be recognized for what it is, simply a put-and-take fishery for river systems where angling pressure is severe.

The Sea-Run Cutthroat Trout

On one or two occasions during every steelhead season the angler will strike at the tell-tale dip of his float only to find that he has hooked a small but very active and flashy sea-run cutthroat trout. Much has occurred in the management of this special sports fish during the past two decades including special regulations and enhancement programs. These seem to have turned the tide in favor of this spunky trout, yet much is still to be done if they are to return to their special place in coastal streams.

The sea-run is that special breed of trout which annually or semi-annually journeys up his native stream searching for food, protection, and a suitable habitat for his progeny. Their needs for survival and their potential are still little known. Yet, they have a following of dedicated anglers who credit their sporting qualities as superior even to the wily steelhead.

There are few, if any, coastal anglers who did not learn their stream knowledge and love of angling from this trout. Their earliest childhood angling excursions were likely aimed at baiting bullheads in the tidal marshes, creeks, and streams. But, these early excursions quickly blossomed into bobber and worm-plunking pursuits for that flashy silver trout, the yellow belly. Their adult interests may have shifted to the potency and magnitude of the steelhead or the intriguing challenge of stream coho or chinook but, invariably, at least once or twice a year (usually in April or October), they will revert to a light trout fly rod. In an almost melancholy, yet youthful eagerness they will quietly and skillfully cast to the runs and ripples of their favorite stream for the light tug and aerial battle of this sparkling silver trout.

The knowing steelheader who beaches one of these fish with his heavy gear in December to April will relish the short but extremely pleasurable battle; but, very carefully, he will release this respected adversary so that it can continue on its upstream migration. Fortunately, with recent publicity, more and more anglers are now understanding how scarce these fish have become and that the species needs to be protected and perpetuated.

The sea-run cutthroat trout, yellow belly, tinsel trout, harvest trout, or just sea-run cutt, as it may be affectionately called by anglers, has a life history much like that of the steelhead trout. Entering the rivers in early July through late winter it seeks its small home creek for spawning. It does this in the period between February and May. Only during the actual spawning and for a short time afterward does the sea-run appear thin and emaciated. Recovery from spawning is rapid and, if food is readily available, the fish is soon trim and slick once again. Being true trout, sea-run cutthroat trout do not die after spawning and may return to spawn a second and third time.

The life of the harvest trout begins in the small, bushy streams which are preferred for spawning and as nurseries. These are the small but highly critical tributary creeks which feed every bay, stream, and estuary along the coast. The female normally carries about 1,200 eggs which are deposited in the redd, a nest located in medium, sized gravel. The eggs are bright red-orange in color and about one quarter the size of steelhead eggs. After hatching, the fry will remain in the stream from one to three years, finally migrating to salt water estuaries during spring months when they are ten to twenty centimeters in length. Little is known of their life history in the sea but it is thought that they spend their adult life in the bays and estuaries near their home creek and eventually reach from one to three kilos in weight.

For aesthetic appeal the sea-run is unequalled by any other salmonid. His body color consists of a dark green above, olive green on the sides and silver below. Covering the fish is a basic bright yellow which is dominant on the fins and belly. There is a pinkish sheen on the gill covers and on the fins. Numerous small dark spots on the back, sides, and fins extend well below the lateral line. In fish fresh from the sea, the back tends to a metallic bluish color while the sides have a pronounced silver sheen. His most distinguishing characteristic, however, is the presence of a brilliant red or orange streak along the inner edge of the lower jaw—hence the name cutthroat.

Angling methods for sea-runs vary, with plunkers, bait, lure, and fly-fishermen all taking their share of yellow bellies. Since cutthroat trout remain near the estuaries and bays of their home streams, tidal fishing for cutts is a year-round sport. Tidal fishing usually takes place during any incoming tide and particularly during the evening summer flooding tides.

I would be remiss if I did not share my favorite method, that of fly-fishing, for these spunky trout. A very light outfit with a long rod in the #4 to #6 weight class is ideal. My preference is for a short sinktip fly line with a long leader of at least three meters in length. I have found that a yellow or gold fly like the professor, california, polar coachman or golden thorn, retrieved with a fast strip retrieve is very effective. Other patterns, like a muddler or one with a silver body like the mickey finn, also fill my fly box and have been equally effective.

The season and the type of tackle preferred account for the different names used by anglers for the sea-run cutthroat trout. During April and May, when pink and chum salmon are migrating to the sea, sea-run cutts surge into the streams to devour these silvery smolts. The favored lure of anglers at this time is a silver tinsel fly—hence the name tinsel trout. In the summer and fall when he is hooked in fresh water he is called a yellow belly because of his decidedly yellowish fins and belly. The name harvest trout refers to the October cutts who have entered the streams following the spawning salmon. It seems that most sea-runs will enter streams at this time of the year to gorge on salmon eggs.

The sea-run cutt has received much publicity and protection in recent years. Specific enhancement projects like those on the Oyster River have provided a successful fishery and given much scientific data to fisheries managers. Unquestionably, it is the sea-run's special habitat, the small coastal creeks and stream tributaries, which must be protected if this special sports trout is to ever reach historic numbers and once again provide a viable and enriching angling heritage.

Aesthetic Values

From the riverbank, the steelheader must view clear sparkling water with sufficient seasonal flow to ensure a nursery and shelter for steelhead fry and adults.

Exploitation of the forests or land must not, and I repeat, must not be evident from the stream's edge. There must be a life-line of greenery in its pristine state paralleling the river and its nursery tributaries. It is inconceivable to consider a violation of this, the river's umbilical life-line, for any reason.

The actual presence or signs of wildlife; the impatience of the dipper, the tracks of mammals, the delicacy of a stone fly, the splash of trout are indispensable to deepen the outdoor experience and foster an awareness for the beauty and infinite complexity of nature.

Aesthetic quality will also acknowledge the rights of human endeavor in the utilization of resources. But, there must never be visual evidence of unilateral exploitation or insufficient protection for other resources or users of the land.

Intrinsic Values

Truly it is with the intrinsic values of steelheading that definition is most difficult. These inner values are as infinite as the water molecules in the streams where I fish. Yet, all stream anglers have a common bond which permits the base for communication. This base can best be defined as knowledge:

- Knowledge that success is possible and probable.

- Knowledge that the river's triangle—its nursery watershed, its river highway, and its irreplaceable estuary are protected and managed for the benefit of all resource users.

- Knowledge that resource users recognize their land stewardship and actively provide adequate protection as well as initiative for new procedures.

- Knowledge of laws for the protection of his sport.

- Knowledge of management programs for the enhancement of his sport.

- Knowledge and confidence in his ability to change these laws or alter these programs.

- Knowledge that access is unrestricted both for the fish and himself.

The angler is the river guardian. Maintenance of river quality is also his responsibility. This requires a knowledge of the life history and habitat requirements of his sports fish. It also commands the concept of an environment left as it was found, unlittered, untarnished and enhanced by his presence.

The Steelheader

The Steelheader is a highly specialized sports fisherman who, because of the very nature of steelhead, must become involved with the river environment where he pursues his trophy. This relationship, as well as requiring a primary knowledge of the basic life history of his fish, also requires an intimate knowledge of every pool and run, every access point and game trail and every mood and change in the flow and quality of the river water.

The Steelheader is extremely possessive of his home stream—that stream on which he will spend well over half of a season's angling hours fishing. When any abnormal factor intrudes upon the angler's intimate knowledge of his stream he is piqued to immediate action.

It is in action that the Steelheader shows the depth of his involvement and reverence for his trophy trout. And, it is action which differentiates the Steelheader from the river angler.

Occasionally, the action taken appears unsuccessful in the eyes of the Steelheader. It leads to frustration, anger, delays, and eventually a care-not attitude. It leads to a need for personal immunity from future desecrations to his home stream. Enter then the period of nostalgia, the longing for things that used to be, the angler-senility.

Like his home river, which every season must be learned anew; where the fish holts are; where the new slicks and lies exist; and, where the variables of nature, the game trails and beaver dams have altered stream flows and angler trails, so must the Steelheader recognize the fatality of angler senility.

It is his fish and his stream which needs protection and this will only be if he is willing to accept natural change and fight unnatural desecration. The viability and variability of his fish, the steelhead, will assure the continuation of his sport providing that the watershed nurseries and the natural stream habitat are protected. The steelhead is a barometer of a healthy natural stream environment and it must be the Steelheader's responsibility to make it axiomatic that the steelhead be recognized as the barometer of a healthy stream.

The frustrations often experienced by Steelheaders need not be if the angler has the initiative to be organized to rectify the situations that lead to a lessening of the quality of his sport. And, contrary to popular belief, being organized does not necessitate belonging to any specific organization or fishing club, although there is no doubt that there is strength in group action. Rather, though, it is personal organization which can lead to the right action at the right time.

Often Steelheaders would like the opportunity to actively participate in some phase of stream management but are unable to commit themselves to the time restrictions of group projects. For these Steelheaders whose interest and affection for a stream stems from their association with water, fish, or the streamside environment, the Stream Guardian role is aptly suited. On their time they can adopt a specific stream and carry out numerous projects which will preserve wildlife habitat, salmonid enhancement and stream rehabilitation.

The intimate knowledge that the Steelheader accumulates from personal experiences, records, and observations can provide a barometer of the basic ecology of that stream and of the effects of changes on the integrity of that stream. This knowledge is vital as a benchmark for management programs and regulations as is his individual expertise with the stream. If the Steelheader is an ardent outdoor enthusiast, the emotions he feels for his stream will ensure on-stream education for all he meets, to protect and perpetuate his fish and his stream.

Appendix

British Columbia Steelhead Catch Statistical Graphs

Since 1968, the Fish & Wildlife Branch of the Ministry of Environment, Lands and Parks has kept an analysis of the steelhead sports catch on the over 450 listed steelhead streams in British Columbia. The first statistics covered the 1967/68 steelhead season (Steelhead Trout Sport Fishery Analysis 1967/68 by G. R. Peterson and R. C. Thomas, Fisheries Management Report No. 59, 1968) and listed, at that time, approximately 250 B.C. steelhead streams. Since that time, as access to other streams has occurred and as tributary streams have been catalogued as bearing steelhead, the Fisheries Branch has labelled 451 known recreational steelhead angling streams in the province.

For the purpose of general information for the readers I have concentrated my charts and data on the time period covering the 1981/82 angling period through to the 1990/91 season, a ten year period of time when steelhead angling questionnaire statistics were all catalogued in a similar manner. Since that period, there have been alterations in methods of collecting data with the result that comparable data is not possible and can be confusing. Readers unfamiliar with British Columbia steelhead should note that steelhead sports fish licenses cover the time period from April 1 through to March 31 of the following year. Hence, we have a steelheading season covering time in two calendar years.

I have started with the 1981/82 season for my charts as this is the first season where hatchery caught steelhead were included in the summary statistics. The season 1990/91 has been used as the conclusion simply because the next season, 1991/92, did not include a sample of nonresident Canadians, which consitutes a large number of anglers, and hence was not comparable to the previous ten years. Later usable data was not available at the writing of this text due to government budget reductions.

I have found writing and preparing the value section extremely distasteful for how can one place a dollar value on something as intrinsic as the sport of steelheading. Even more distasteful is the placement of a dollar value on a steelhead. Yet, through the years of championing our trophy sports trout, I have been repeatedly asked those very questions by business and, yes, even by various governments.

Surprisingly, (or not, depending upon which side you take) it has only been in recent years that commercial steelhead catch statistics have become public knowledge. Now, having access to these figures, I have compiled graphs to give steelhead anglers a tragic look at what has happened to our trophy trout.

Precise details of every stream for the past three decades are available from the Fisheries Branch of the Ministry of Environment, Lands and Parks in Victoria or from regional offices. Specific information on the steelhead commercial catch can be obtained from the Ministry of Fisheries and Oceans in Ottawa.

1. Top Twenty B.C. Steelhead Rivers by Catch: 1990-91

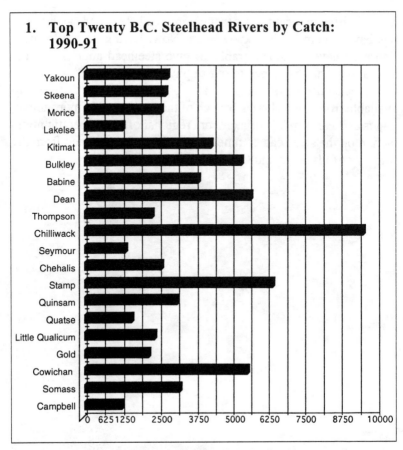

B.C. Ministry of Environment, Lands & Parks, Fisheries Branch

Graph by Barry Thornton

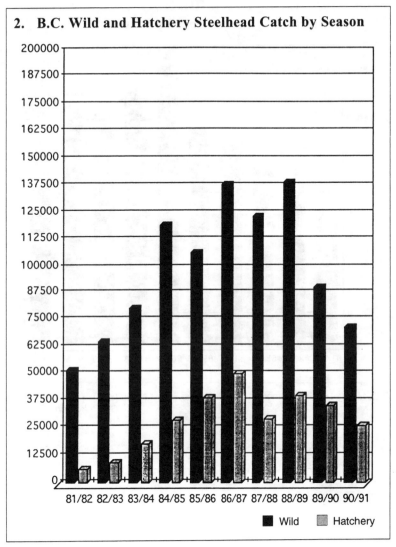

2. B.C. Wild and Hatchery Steelhead Catch by Season

B.C. Ministry of Environment, Lands & Parks, Fisheries Branch

Graph by Barry Thornton

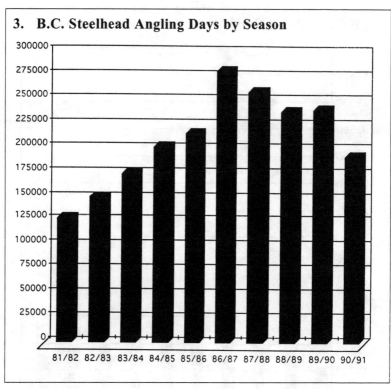

3. B.C. Steelhead Angling Days by Season

B.C. Ministry of Environment, Lands & Parks, Fisheries Branch

Graph by Barry Thornton

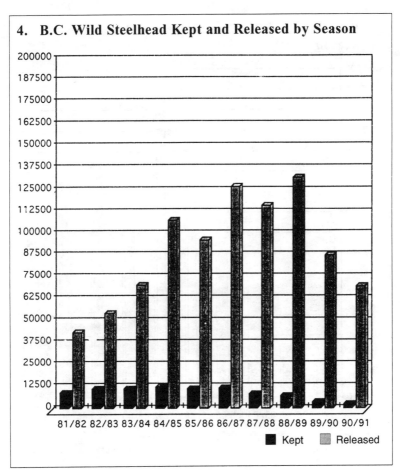

4. B.C. Wild Steelhead Kept and Released by Season

B.C. Ministry of Environment, Lands & Parks, Fisheries Branch

Graph by Barry Thornton

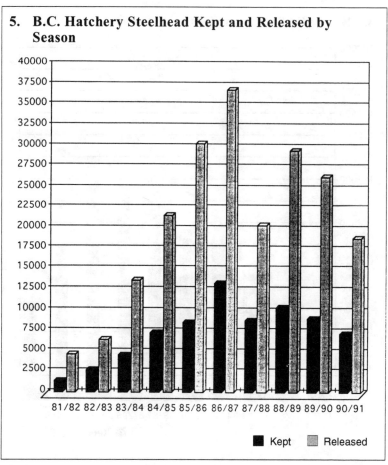

5. B.C. Hatchery Steelhead Kept and Released by Season

B.C. Ministry of Environment, Lands & Parks, Fisheries Branch

Graph by Barry Thornton

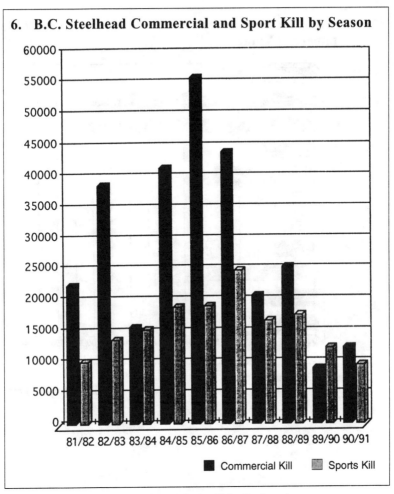

6. B.C. Steelhead Commercial and Sport Kill by Season

Legend: ■ Commercial Kill   ▨ Sports Kill

B.C. Ministry of Environment, Lands & Parks, Fisheries Branch
Salmonid Enhancement Program   *Graph by Barry Thornton*

7. Multiple Times Steelhead Sport Value Has Exceeded Commercial Value

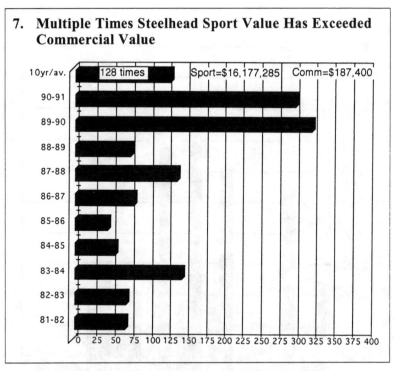

B.C. Ministry of Environment, Lands & Parks, Fisheries Branch
S.E.P., Ministry Fisheries & Oceans   *Graph by Barry Thornton*

8. Vancouver Island Top Ten Steelhead Rivers by Catch: 1991-92 Season

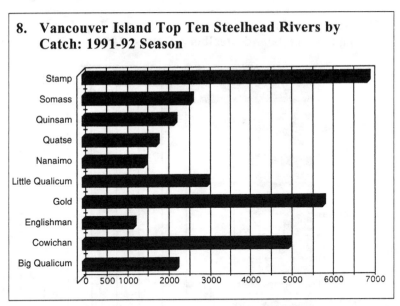

B.C. Ministry of Environment, Lands & Parks, Fisheries Branch

Graph by Barry Thornton

9. Ten Year Average Value of Commercial and Sport Steelhead: 1981-82 to 1990-91

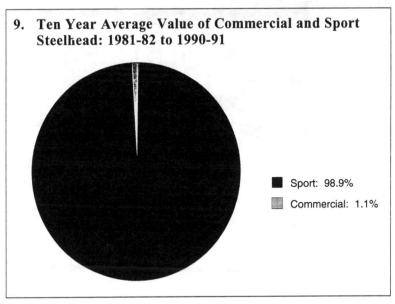

B.C. Ministry of Environment, Lands & Parks, Fisheries Branch
S.E.P., Ministry of Fisheries & Oceans   *Graph by Barry Thornton*

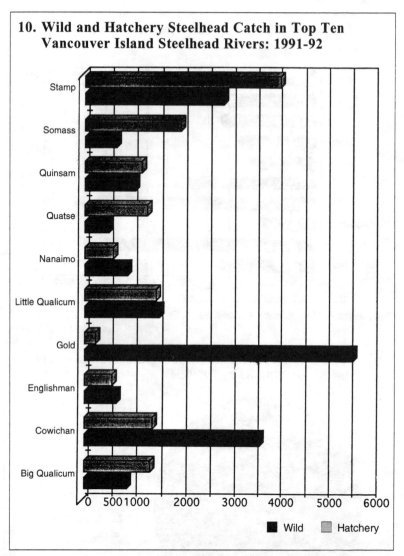

10. Wild and Hatchery Steelhead Catch in Top Ten Vancouver Island Steelhead Rivers: 1991-92

B.C. Ministry of Environment, Lands & Parks, Fisheries Branch

Graph by Barry Thornton

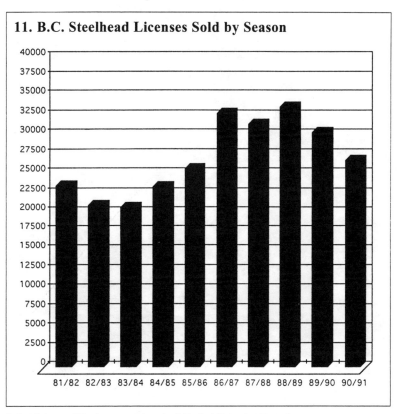

11. B.C. Steelhead Licenses Sold by Season

B.C. Ministry of Environment, Lands & Parks, Fisheries Branch

Graph by Barry Thornton

Quality Hancock House Titles

The Last Cast
Fishing Reminiscences
Rafe Mair
ISBN 0-88839-346-6

Saltwater Fly Fishing
for Pacific Salmon
Barry M. Thornton
ISBN 0-88839-268-0

Mooching
The Salmon
Fisherman's Bible
David Nuttall
ISBN 0-88839-097-1

Trout Fishing
The Tactical Secrets
of Lake Fishing
Ed Rychkun
ISBN 0-88839-338-5

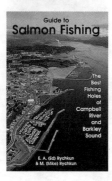

Guide to Salmon Fishing
The Best Fishing Holes of
Campbell River & Barkley
Sound
Ed Rychkun
ISBN 0-88839-305-9

West Coast River Angling
Eric Carlisle
ISBN 0-88839-212-5

Available from Hancock House Publishers
USA: 1431 Harrison Avenue, Blaine, WA 98230-5005
Canada: 19313 Zero Avenue, Surrey, B.C. V4P 1M7
For orders call: 1-800-938-1114 Fax: 1-800-983-2262
Credit cards accepted. Business line: (604) 538-1114

Unsolicited manuscripts accepted for consideration.